Praise for
Discovering Agreement

If we seek peace and community in the world, strangely enough, lawyers will lead us there, specifically through the restorative framework and movement. Discovering Agreement is a brilliant book. One basic insight is that if we can look at, versus look through, the framework in which we create contracts and disputes, it changes everything. The shift from prediction and control to sense and respond is decisive. The author writes easily about a worldview whose ideas are grounded and accessible. The book changes the way we connect with each other and comes at this from the backdoor, where your lawyer is your best friend and the best friend of those you thought were on the other side. Six stars in a five-star world.

Peter Block, consultant, author, and citizen of Cincinnati

In this delightfully readable and important book, Linda Alvarez shows us how to transcend the narrow confines of conventional thinking about contracts and contract law to carve out a new approach based on value creation, sustainability, and resilience. This can help us attain the much desired but seldom attained 'simplicity on the other side of complexity' that the famed jurist Oliver Wendell Holmes, Jr. spoke of. I expect that the ideas put forth in *Discovering Agreement* are essential to building and leading conscious businesses.

Raj Sisodia, Professor of Global Business, Babson College; Co-Founder and Co-Chairman of the Board, Conscious Capitalism; Co-Author, *Conscious Capitalism Liberating the Heroic Spirit of Business*

D1590765

Linda Alvarez's readable and thoughtful book is a marvel. It focuses on contracts and disputes—staple articles of law practice—and gives many valuable insights and a fresh perspective on how lawyers and clients should approach them. She articulates how conscious practices by lawyers and clients can improve contract formation—which she explains as the building and structuring of relationships within legal frameworks—as well as the anticipation and handling of conflicts that arise from them. She challenges complacency in a world of brittle negotiations and disputes, providing not only lofty principles but detailed practical advice for immediate and effective reform. It is a must-read both for lawyers who need to step back from their daily grind to find more satisfying outcomes for their clients (and themselves) and for law students who can compare this fresh approach with the traditional concepts about negotiation, contracts, and disputes that they are learning in law school. And it may also bring more happiness and professional fulfillment to practitioners who adopt its approach.

Andrew P. Bridges, Fenwick & West LLP, Partner
Litigation, Co-chair Copyright Litigation

Law students rave about *Discovering Agreement*. It gives them permission to think big, to expand their vision of what it means to be a lawyer, to reignite the creativity and optimism that led them to pursue a legal education. "We lawyers sometimes forget," writes Linda Alvarez, "how much leeway the parties have to design their own legal systems." Her book is a reminder and a path-breaking guide for how parties can use contracts not as "weapons of war," but as catalysts for peace. *Discovering Agreement* is also a tool for empowerment and self-determination. It invites us to relinquish the image of transactional lawyers as cogs in a machine, driven by fear and risk aversion, replacing it with a vision of lawyers as constructive collaborators. Alvarez embodies "mindfulness in action" at its best: she models humility, integrity, and deep wisdom as practices that can be integrated into the core commitments of a professional life. A must-read for any lawyer, law professor, or law student who wishes to join the movement that is turning the legal profession into a compassionate, enlightened calling.

Shari Motro, Professor of Law, University of Richmond

Linda Alvarez's conflict resolution method in her groundbreaking book *Discovering Agreement* has been an endless source of guidance for my startup team here at Wevorce. I expect Linda's book will soon become required reading for every entrepreneur. Gone will be the habitual, lethal spiral of confrontation that often goes hand-in-hand with disputes in the fast-paced, pressure-cooker world of startup entrepreneurship. Instead, a road-tested, reliable, legally enforceable alternative that generates a positive and productive path will take its place. This conscientious new path will inspire greater creativity and productivity, resilience in the face of conflict and change, and an end to the pitfalls and molasses-slow pace of conventional legal practices.

Michelle Crosby, founder & CEO, Wevorce

Discovering Agreement

Contracts That Turn Conflict Into Creativity

by

Linda Alvarez

CANDESCENCE MEDIA

Cover design by Carolyn Sexton

The materials contained herein represent the opinions of the authors and/or the editors, and should not be construed to be the views or opinions of the law firms or companies with whom such persons are in partnership, associated, or employed by.

Nothing contained in this book is to be considered as the rendering of legal advice for specific cases, and readers are responsible for obtaining such advice from their own legal counsel. This book is intended for educational and informational purposes only.

ISBN: 978-0-9993292-0-7
e-ISBN: 978-0-9993292-1-4

Discounts are available for books ordered in bulk.
Inquire at info@CandescenceMedia.com.

CONTENTS

About Linda   i
Acknowledgments   iii
Introduction: My Story   vi

SECTION I   15
Chapter 1   The World in Which We Find Ourselves   17
Chapter 2   Evolving Business Realities and Mindsets   31
Chapter 3   Cause of Action   45
Chapter 4   Introducing Discovering Agreement   55

SECTION II   73
Chapter 5   Touchstone   75
Chapter 6   Addressing Change & Engaging Disagreement   93
Chapter 7   Lawyers and Clients   117
Chapter 8   Playing Well with Others   141
Chapter 9   Reflections   159

Works Cited   179
Appendix: Samples and Examples   189

About Linda

The first twenty years of Linda Alvarez's professional life were spent pursuing a successful career in the arts. Trained in theater, she and her husband produced and managed theatrical and media productions across the United States. In the mid-1990s, Linda reentered the academic world earning her law degree, magna cum laude, in 1997. She entered private practice in the large-firm environment—including Wilson Sonsini Goodrich & Rosati (Palo Alto) and Vinson & Elkins (Houston). Later, as senior counsel for litigation and trademarks at Align Technology, Inc., Linda managed litigations on behalf of the corporation as well as shepherding the company's valuable consumer trademark portfolio. Linda launched her solo practice in 2005 and, in 2012, was recognized by the American Bar Association as a "legal rebel" for her innovative approach to contract formation.

Linda developed Discovering Agreement as a way to reframe the negotiation process, the drafting of contract language, and the performance of contractual relationships. Where conventional perspectives cast the parties as adversaries and bargaining power as a function of dominance, Discovering Agreement orients the parties as collaborators codesigning their ideal business relationship. With Discovering Agreement, parties take the reins and, facilitated by legal counsel, build their own ideal systems within the context of the larger legal-justice system, actively transforming how the conventional system impacts their present and future interactions and dealings.

Linda's approach grew out of years of study of the principles of active and effective nonviolence and draws on proven mediation and restorative justice models of dispute resolution. It is also informed by current research in neuroscience, and by developing trends in business, such as "Conscious Capitalism" (reorienting business governance and development towards socially, environmentally, and personally responsible values).

Acknowledgments

I am grateful to so many people—family, friends, and colleagues—for their generous and crucial support as this book was coming into being.

I'll begin with my family. Thank you to my sisters: Deeanne Gist, the bestselling author with a veritable library of ten acclaimed novels to her name, has been a stabilizing and reassuring presence whenever my confidence wavered, and Gayle Evers has rescued me with moral, editorial, and technical support that I could not have done without. Seriously, had it not been for Gayle's efforts, I might still be sitting at the keyboard. And, of course, thank you to my heroic husband, Richard Alvarez, an award-winning screenwriter and also a novelist, who has been a sounding board, a faithful reader, and a calming voice when I flirted with panic over deadlines and expectations.

I cannot separate the categories "friends" and "colleagues" and that makes me a very lucky woman indeed. The list of those who have contributed to making the book possible is extensive, and I am sure to be still thinking of names long after the date of publication. J. Kim Wright has been my daily "writing buddy" commiserating and cheerleading via texts, e-mail, Skype, and telephone. She is also an inspiration as an indefatigable leader of the Integrative Law Movement. Glenn Meier generously shared his own experiences and allowed me to share them with you through his contribution to this book. Jenna Andres provided comprehensive and wonderfully precise editorial support at a crucial moment in the book's formation. Others who have read various drafts and given their feedback, helping bring clarity to the work, include Marjorie Florestal, Mary Russell, Mika Dashman, Shoshanna Silverberg, Chris Tittle, Annabelle Berrios, and Shari Motro. Moral support that energized me when my spirit flagged was also provided by my beloved friends Rhonni Dubose and Phil Perry, and by wonderful colleagues: Hass Sadeghi, Jeena Cho, Ngoc Nguyen, Seth Weiner, and Wevorce founder, Michelle Crosby, as well as Chris Zydel who gave me sanctuary in her Creative Juices Arts Studio during the last intensive weeks of writing this book.

I would also like to acknowledge the shoulders on which this work stands. Those intrepid souls who have courageously lived the principles of nonviolence in the midst of conflict, who have made it their life's work to help others engage conflict restoratively and creatively, and who have shared what they learned. I owe a deep debt of gratitude to Marshall Rosenberg who developed a practice he called Nonviolent Communication. Attending his trainings and reading his books blew my mind and gave me hope when I needed it most. Dominic Barter, who calls his work "Restorative Circles," is a personal hero of mine. I never pass up the opportunity to listen to Dominic speak or to attend a workshop he is presenting. I learn so much just by watching how Dominic lives the principles of nonviolence and responds restoratively and compassionately in emotionally charged situations where the rest of us are cringing and running for cover.

An early resource in my search for a new way to approach the tensions inherent in contract negotiation and enforcement was Stewart Levine. His books, *The Book of Agreement and Getting to Resolution*, were beacons lighting a path for me to a new way of being in the practice of law. Gary Freidman and Jack Himmelstein's "Understanding in Conflict" mediation model, with its long-track record of success, has blazed a trail in alternative dispute resolution, offering a robust and reliable process for helping those locked in painful conflict to create lasting and meaningful resolution. It is my go-to backup system for engaging conflict productively, and I highly recommend the trainings and other programs offered by The Center for

Understanding in Conflict. Finally, I thank John O'Donohue, the Irish poet, philosopher, and author, for placing me at the threshold where I had to find a new way of engaging life's challenges and for providing the inspiration that continues to light my way.

Introduction: My Story

The radio report of the second tower's collapse came as I was turning into the office parking garage at the end of my morning commute. I rode the elevator to the 25th floor, picked up my computer, told my secretary to go home, and left the office. The tragedy of all those people whose lives ended so suddenly in their offices stunned me, and in the mental stillness that followed, a question I could not ignore began to grow in my mind. Was my legal practice the work I wanted to be doing on the day I died? September 11, 2001 was the last day I was able to kid myself about how I felt practicing law.

I'd been working as an associate in big law firms since my graduation from law school four years earlier. A highly effective advocate, I often joked with colleagues and clients that the opposition had no chance; we would "squish 'em like a bug." At the same time, anxiety had become a constant in my life, like a low-grade fever I could never really shake off. There was plenty to love about the job. The pay was great. I was good at what I did. Clients loved me. I got along well with colleagues. But I felt an ever-increasing uneasiness in my role as enforcer and combatant.

September 11, 2001 was also a first day. It was the day I started to really study the relationship between power and violence.

In the aftermath of the 9/11 attacks, the escalating military response seemed to beget more violence rather than end it. Hate seemed to be growing, not diminishing. But what was the alternative? Was there any way to respond that might disarm rather than escalate hatred and violence? Was it possible to respond to horrific violence in a powerful way without becoming perpetrators of harm ourselves? I began to think about Gandhi—an example of powerful nonviolence, "powerful" because his approach was effective to obtain results. Remembering Gandhi was a contemporary of Hitler, I started searching for what he had said about nonviolence in response to Nazi atrocities.

Gandhi believed a violent response will always have a cost. When asked, he said a nonviolent response could, eventually, end the Nazi horrors, but that many, many people would die in the meantime. And he said something more. He said that while a nonviolent response is always better (because it does not carry within it the seeds for retaliation and further violence), if one is not capable of responding nonviolently, then one should take whatever measures necessary—even violent ones—to stop injustice.[1]

He named his approach to power and nonviolence by coining the word, "satyagraha." The word itself holds the key to Gandhi's approach. "Satya" means "truth" and "agraha" means "hold tight."[2] For him, the power of nonviolence was rooted in the principle and practice of "holding tight to truth."

The more I learned about nonviolent principles and practices, the more I became convinced that a truly nonviolent response is the most powerful and effective way to end injustice and engage conflict. In the course of my studies, I witnessed nonviolent responses to harm bringing healing, restoring relationships and a

---

[1] "He who cannot protect himself or his nearest and dearest or their honor by non-violently facing death may and ought to do so by violently dealing with the oppressor. He who can do neither of the two is a burden." Gandhi, and Thomas Merton. "Section Two, Non-Violence: True and False." *Gandhi on Non-violence: Selected Texts from Mohandas K. Gandhi's Non-violence in Peace and War*. New York: New Directions Pub., 2007. p.50. Print (citing Gandhi. Non-violence in Peace & War. Vol. 1. Ahmedabad: Navajivan, 1944. Print.)

[2] Nagler, Michael N. *The Nonviolence Handbook: A Guide for Practical Action*. Berrett-Koehler, 2014. Print.; Gandhi, and Thomas Merton. "Section Two, Non-Violence: True and False." *Gandhi on Nonviolence: Selected Texts from Mohandas K. Gandhi's Non-violence in Peace and War*. New York: New Directions Pub., 2007. p.4. Print.

trustworthy foundation for community and safety.

But believing and practicing were a world apart from one another. As a lawyer—living in the arena of conflict—I hated the bullying. I hated being bullied, and I hated being a bully. And it was my job to not only be a bully, but a paranoid one. It seemed to me that "truth" was not a useful word in the legal field. Truth is subjective, so we assume it is pointless to try and figure out what is true. We focus instead upon what we can get for the client. We understand "power" as being the ability to dominate and control a situation or outcome. We keep our eye on how to protect self and client while controlling the actions and choices of others.

Eventually, I left the Big Firm culture and took a position as inhouse counsel at a corporation where I managed litigations on behalf of the company. I spent my days battling in the conventional system using conventional tactics. Often the conduct of the lawyers for the other side appalled me. What was right and what was civil seemed to be of very little interest to many. It was disheartening. What was worse, the system itself supported, even encouraged, this gamesmanship and tactical escalation over problem solving and resolution.

I felt like my life was running along two completely separate tracks. On one track, I was still the "squish 'em like a bug" lawyer, engaging conflict on behalf of clients and playing the zero-sum "we win/you lose" game. On the other track, I was striving to conduct my personal life according to the principles of nonviolence. I was practicing empathy, compassion, and vulnerability as ways to create a better world—except for the hours and energy I still dedicated to the conventional legal culture and system. The deeper my personal commitment to nonviolence, the greater my anxiety became over the disconnect between my deeply held values and the work I was doing.

Then one day, during my morning commute, I caught myself fantasizing about having an automobile accident and being injured "just enough" to prevent me from having to go to the law office ever again. I was stunned, so stunned that for a moment my mind came to a complete halt. Happily, my next thought was, "I can wish for something better than that!"

A short time later, I quit my job. I believed I was leaving the law. My plan (literally) was to get a job at a bookstore, so I started slashing expenses. I moved my family out of our three-bedroom, two-bath home with a yard and a gate letting out to the park. I rented a tiny two-bedroom, one-bath apartment, gave up my Blackberry, and started teaching knitting at the local yarn shop.

I kept one client—on the condition that I was not expected to do any enforcement or litigation work. And then, magically, the author, philosopher, and poet, John O'Donohue, hired me to take over as his business manager. Perfect. It was a nonlawyer gig, and it was work that I could believe in. I would be working with John as he created new works (books, films, and the like) and brought his message of deep spirituality (through speaking and conducting retreats) to an ever-growing audience. I started on June 1, 2007. New life, here I come! Then, on January 3, 2008, John died unexpectedly in his sleep. At the age of 52, this robust and vibrant man's heart gave out, and he was gone.

I felt betrayed by fate. It just wasn't possible that he was gone. Losing John and the future I'd been so eagerly entering was enough to create an undercurrent of anger in my being. To then discover there were people taking advantage of his absence to generate money for themselves using his work was enough to bring out the roaring legal-beast.

Many of these people counted themselves as John's friends. John counted them as friends. How could they do this to him and his family? I started firing off stern demand letters. The responses appalled me. People I knew were infringing John's rights claimed that their efforts were meant to honor John, and they accused me of behaving in ways that did not comport with his message and work. As anger on both sides escalated, my distress rose along with it. Going to war was clearly not getting me closer to the goal of protecting and preserving John's rights. The harder I tried to do the right thing, the farther outside John's circle of love and care everyone seemed to go.

It was incredibly painful and not particularly productive. In all practicality, litigation was not an attractive option for John's family. They were utterly shattered and just trying to breathe through bleak days of loss and sorrow. The estate was tangled up in the legal quagmire that accompanies sudden and unexpected death. Something other than the conventional approach was needed. So I dragged my mind away from my justifiable indignation, stepped back from my lawyerly habits, and tried to "hold tight to truth."

The truth was, these people loved John. It was highly unlikely that they would intentionally harm him or his family. Another truth was, these relationships were as important to the future of John's work as were the rights I was trying to protect. It was imperative that I did not destroy one in order to preserve the other. Yet, as long as we were on opposite sides, lobbing accusations at one another and clinging to our righteous anger, there would be no hope of bringing a harmonious result.

Even in this role as business manager, I was acting out the legal training that had me primed to vanquish the opponent. I was in love with my righteous indignation. Society doesn't advocate stepping into the shoes of what menaces us, doesn't teach us to seek an understanding of our opponent for purposes other than exploitation. Most people would say that empathy for the other side is not a characteristic they desire in their representative. I was stepping out into new territory. Instead of relying solely on my legal training, I applied the principles and practices of nonviolence. It was one of the hardest things I've ever tried to do—to look at the situation from the point of view of my enemy.

And then, I stopped seeing an enemy. My approach to these difficult conversations changed. It began with curiosity about what was driving other people's choices. Once they realized I was genuinely interested in understanding their point of view, the other parties began to relax. By connecting with them at the point where they were most invested, I found I was able to open a meaningful dialogue. By "dialogue" I do not mean negotiation. Negotiations tend to be serial monologues with each speaker only listening to the other for the purpose of preparing a rebuttal or manipulative response. By contrast, dialogue is a conversation where participants are actively engaged in seeking mutual understanding, in trying to convey and receive true meaning. Dominic Barter, a well-known teacher (and he would insist student) of nonviolence, uses "dialogue" to mean, a nonhierarchical conversation among equals with no known outcome, conducted with willingness to be influenced and changed by what we hear.[3] I found that my willingness to look at things from other people's point of view, to sincerely try to understand their interests and needs, opened in them a reciprocal willingness to listen and understand why their actions were triggering objections from the estate.

It is never easy, in midst of a conflict, to drop the idea that the other party is an opponent. I was far from adept. I still feel angry when I look back at some of the situations, and I feel some regret for my own lack of skill in handling them at that early stage. But I learned from every experience, and each time a similar situation arose I did a little better. I stopped my "identify and hate the enemy" game a little sooner each time and began to enter conversations by expressing and reminding everyone of the love we shared for John and his work, and the vision we all wanted serve to further his message—aside from, while still including, our separate needs and desires. This was the practicum in "holding tight to truth"— my truth and theirs.

Taking this approach interrupted the attack/counterattack pattern, allowing everyone to begin releasing their

[3] Barter, Dominic. "DominicBarterJune12015." *SoundCloud*. Keynote Speech, Nat'l Assoc. of Community and Restorative Justice, 1 June 2015. Web. 25 Aug. 2015.

defensiveness. Starting from a point of shared values and vision oriented us as partners in cocreating a future we all desired rather than as adversaries battling for opposing positions. We were better able to listen carefully, clarify the needs, goals, and visions we each held, identify which were being served and which were not, and then codesign agreements that worked for everyone without sacrificing or betraying anyone's core values and visions.

After one such reparative conversation, I sat down to write the contract memorializing the agreement we had reached. This time instead of starting with the typical "Recitations" ("WHEREAS the Party of the First Part desires...; and WHEREAS the Party of the Second Part is willing..."), I wrote a brief statement about the parties' shared love and respect for John and his work, and about the intentions we all held that were foundational to the agreement we had reached. Including this statement in the written contract meant that it would be there if we ever again found ourselves in a heated disagreement.

Then, I went one step further. In place of a boilerplate arbitration clause, I substituted a provision I named, "Addressing Change and Engaging Disagreement." In this clause I expressed the parties' mutual commitment to meet disruptive change and disagreement by seeking collaborative transformation directed at restoring and maintaining alignment of our actions with the love and vision described in the contract's recitations.

In short, the contract language included a built-in system for calling on our better angels. We could—and did—use it as our navigational guide for decision making and resolution of disagreement and to answer enemy images and outrage with reminders of what we shared and our mutual commitment to using that shared love and vision.

I began calling this new process for forming, drafting, and enforcing contracts, "Discovering Agreement." It is a process where the parties are not duking it out to win the deal or negotiate concessions. It is a process of discovering where the parties are already in agreement and where they can adjust actions and plans, so agreement and harmony are enhanced, sustained, and—if needed—restored even in the face of disruptive change or painful conflict.

The practice of Discovering Agreement has enabled me to continue to practice law—as a Satyagrahi. My public/work life and my interior/ personal life are no longer on separate tracks. Being a powerful advocate for my clients does not require sacrificing my principles or betraying my deeply held values.

This book is about the Discovering Agreement process—how it works, how it can be integrated into the practice of law, and what I have learned as I applied the principles and process of nonviolence to all of my work for clients and for myself. It is about a new way to approach contracts and contractual relationships—a new way to have the conversation.

SECTION I

This section explores the world in which we find ourselves, asking how and to what extent conventional systems, practices and mindsets are serving their true purposes in a radically new landscape of incessant technological and cultural shifts. Through the lens of business adaptation and innovation, we'll consider how legal practices are falling short and can be updated and redesigned to better serve clients' changing needs and marketplace realities--in particular, as relates to contracts and business relationships.

CHAPTER 1

The World in Which
We Find Ourselves

People who embark on legal careers almost universally do so because they envision a better world. They see a wrong that needs to be righted and believe they can help bring positive change through their work and expertise. This dedication to pursuing and achieving a better world is what gives meaning to their work. But often they find, no matter what their level of expertise or dedication, "The System" is structured and functioning as an obstacle rather than a vehicle for positive change. Lawyers and their clients routinely rant about the legal system, contracts, and courts, and how the legal system negatively impacts business and personal relationships, goals, and success.

Changing the Conversation

My client, J_____, was beaming as he introduced me to his buddy, "This is Linda, our lawyer. She did our contract with K_____"

J_____'s smile evaporated when his friend replied, "I hope you never have to use it."

The emotion in his reply told me that this man was speaking from harsh experience—the experience of trying to use contract terms and conditions to achieve safety and restore harmony.

If "using" the contract is a miserable eventuality, best avoided, why do we have them? Contracts should be helpful and positive. They should provide frameworks and systems for success. The general dread and distaste with which people approach contract formation and enforcement indicates that something has gone seriously wrong. This, in a nutshell, is why we need a new conversation about contracts.

In the current conversation, we start from the premise that the parties are opponents engaged in competition. Deal-making is approached as an adversarial proceeding, with each party trying to win an advantage over the other. Never mind that the parties are in negotiation because they want to form a working relationship for mutually beneficial purposes. Lawyers talk about "winning the deal" and characterize their role as representing their client "against" the other party. Bargaining power is understood as the ability to dominate the situation and coerce the other party. We expect each side to fight for a greater share of benefits while trying to shift the burden of loss and risk onto their counterpart. The whole process is typically treated as a zero-sum game where any gain by one side imposes an equivalent loss on the other.

The contract document is considered the expression of the parties' relationship, comprising hard-fought deal points and whatever weapons and shelters the lawyers have managed to embed in the boilerplate (those murky paragraphs usually disregarded by the parties and left to the lawyers to parse and haggle over). If either party feels there is an uneven distribution of benefits or risks, then the relationship is experienced as one-up/one-down. The parties begin performance of their contractual obligations with at least one of them operating under the bruised certainty that they have lost something in the negotiation.

The lingering impact of this adversarial process is that the parties have formed a relationship based on scorekeeping and often have established characterizations of the other party as uncooperative, unfair, or bullying. Frequently, both parties feel they've been taken advantage of, and this can trigger a tendency to look for ways to get back at the other, perhaps by giving only the barest minimum performance or by gaming the contractual language to circumvent what one perceives as an unfair requirement.

By casting deal-making as an interaction between opposing parties and memorializing the adversarial culture in the contract language, seeds of future dissent and conflict are planted in the parties' founding interactions and document. When you think about it from a "nonlegal" perspective, it seems like a pretty a lousy way to begin a relationship.

There is, of course, legitimate tension between the interests of two parties when they are striking a bargain. We form cooperative business relationships to improve our position and performance in a competitive marketplace, and in almost every instance there is a balance that must be struck between cooperation and self-interest. Within these cooperative relationships, each of us remains wary of that ephemeral boundary between what is good for the overall, collective effort and what is best for ourselves as individuals. This inherent "Me vs. Us" tension puts plenty of strain on the cohesion and harmony needed to make the relationship work smoothly even before we engage in the conventional adversarial process of contract negotiation and drafting.

Contract law is designed to provide a structure and system for managing these tensions and dealing with the conflicts that arise in human cooperation. But how well is our current system serving the needs contracts are intended to meet? The system and its underlying mindset are so deeply engrained in our collective psyche that we have ceased to notice them, much less question whether the contracting process is all it could be.

Expectations Versus Reality

From the business point of view, the overarching purpose of the contract is to create safety for the parties in their working relationship and shared endeavor. The document's technical goal is to define a set of legally enforceable duties, rights, and promises that the parties have consented to undertake, exchange, and be bound by. A written contract is the mechanism the parties use to establish clarity, predictability, and accountability—allowing everyone involved to enter the bargain with confidence and a sense of security.

Typically, the parties just assume that the existing legal system adequately supports this sense of confidence and security. They file the contract away and go about their daily business, making decisions on the fly, responding to a dynamic marketplace, and taking whatever actions make the most sense in the given moment with available information. Only when a problem arises does the contract come out of the drawer.

When the parties find themselves embroiled in a difficult conversation or set of circumstances, it quickly becomes apparent that "The System" has critical limitations and deficiencies. In practice, clarity is rarely a hallmark of business contracts, predictability is impossible in today's fast-paced, disruptive marketplace, and using the legal system to impose accountability is incredibly slow, expensive, quixotic, and destructive.

When trouble does rear its ugly head, everyone starts scouring the contract language, comparing the agreed course of action with what has actually taken place, keeping score to see which party has wandered farthest (or most profoundly) from the stated terms. The parties may face changes in the law or changes in circumstances that no one anticipated at the time the contract was created. Usually, they discover that no one has been following it completely, and even if they think they have, the meaning of the contract's terms is open to conflicting interpretations.

Contract language is parsed, spun, stretched, and twisted in lawyerly gamesmanship. Arguing about the meaning of the contract language pushes the conversation towards escalating conflict. Assigning blame is essential to knowing who will bear the burden of the loss that looms, and the focus on who is at fault for getting them into this mess increases the parties' polarization. The contract is used in a duel to the death over competing interpretations and counter-accusations of breach. No wonder people hope they never have to use their contracts!

This is not to say that a written contract is worthless. On the contrary, without a written document, the parties run an even greater risk that the legal system will be used to subvert their intentions, destroying relationships and value. Oral agreements can easily devolve into conflicts over existence, interpretation, and enforceability of the most basic terms.

Nevertheless, while it has its good points, the conventional approach undeniably generates toxic by-products. Combative mindsets generate tactics that damage relationships, setting up and perpetuating an adversarial power dynamic between the parties. Negotiation and drafting bog down in acrimonious haggling, and the ultimate document is typically dense with terms and conditions that the parties don't fully comprehend. Lawyers are perceived as a necessary evil, naysaying purveyors of pessimism who taint the parties' relationship with distrust and paranoia.

For lawyers themselves, there is an uncomfortable dissonance between what clients tend to expect (the lawyer will win the deal and create terms that are bulletproof) and the reality of what is possible. Many people delay bringing lawyers into their deal-making conversation out of distaste for the formal negotiation and drafting process. Once the contract is completed, they ignore or hide problems rather than deal with them early on, because pulling the contract out of that file drawer, arguing about interpretation, and casting blame make things worse rather than better. It is a toxic system and cycle.

Taking that rare step backwards and examining the way we approach contract negotiation, drafting, and enforcement reveals the plain reality that the prevailing mindset and procedures are not providing the safety and responsiveness that businesses and individuals have a right to expect. Long adherence to the adversarial mindset has generated a legal system and contractual norms that are neither agile nor efficient. Contractual language is vulnerable to reinterpretation, and litigation processes are slow, expensive, burdensome, and harmful to all parties. Litigation is virtually guaranteed to destroy whatever productive potential might have remained for the contracting parties' relationship and endeavor.

Relinquishing Power

What is more, the conventional process essentially disempowers the parties. Once a contract is created, the parties no longer hold the power over how its language will impact them. A third-party adjudicator has the ultimate power to decide what their contract means and how their conflict will be "resolved." This third-party-decider structure leads to a process of drafting contracts and conducting disputes that emphasizes convincing an outsider to take coercive action on behalf of one party or the other.

The parties, essentially, pour their power into the document and then seal it with their signatures. If a dispute arises that the parties can't resolve on their own, they must go as supplicants to the Great Interpreter (the court of law or arbitration). The adjudicator is the one who unlocks the scope and meaning of the contract terms, wielding the power of interpretation and coercion to impose a prescribed solution—whether the parties are happy with it or not.

The ultimate decision-making power has been deposited in the contract to be extracted by a so-called "disinterested" third party: "The System." But is the system really a disinterested outsider?

Precedent Trumps Practicality

The larger system is not designed to solve the parties' particular problem; the system's function is to dictate an outcome for their dispute. Admittedly, it would be unrealistic to ask the court system to handle the full complexity of real life on a case-by-case basis. The litigation process is already unwieldy and expensive in the extreme.

Over the course of a litigation, each individual case is trimmed of its complexity and is stripped down to its core issues and facts, so it can be correlated to prior cases with the same or similar fact patterns and issues. This trimming and reframing is the locus of the lawyers' and judges' work, and much of the briefing, arguing, and agonizing is focused here. Once an identifiable pattern type emerges, the outcome associated with that pattern type is pulled from legal precedent and imposed on the situation regardless of whether the prescribed result is actually beneficial or wise in the fuller, deeper, particular context of the real-life parties and circumstances. Far too often, abstraction trumps context, reality, and wisdom. Outcomes that are bad for all parties and for the marketplace will be imposed where they satisfy precedent. Parties must be consoled by the assurance that even if the legally correct outcome does not make good sense for their unique situation, the greater good (systemic stability and predictability) has been served.[1]

Predict and Control

We think of dispute resolution as something that takes place after a dispute has arisen, but in actuality, formation and drafting of the contract is a crucial first step in dispute resolution. Contracts are largely treated as tools for predicting and controlling potential conflict and associated risk. The conversation revolves around imagining problems that could arise in the future and negotiating predetermined

---

[1] This has long been identified as a problem in the way our system handles contracts, *see* Holmes, Oliver Wendell, Jr. "The Path of the Law." 10 *Harvard Law Review* 460-61 (1897): 457.

resolutions. Lawyers focus on creating mechanisms for enforcing promises and allocating the burden of loss should the parties face crisis or disagreement down the road.

These prefabricated resolutions are written into the contract with the intent of setting ahead of time the outcome that will be triggered if those particular circumstances arise sometime down the road. But it is impossible to accurately predict and control for all eventualities. The only thing certain is uncertainty. The context during planning can be very different from the context when the terms of the contract are eventually triggered, and what seemed like a great and fair solution at the time the agreement was drafted can turn out to be unrealistic and destructive under new circumstances.

When contract terms are inadequate for managing a crisis or conflict, the parties turn to the legal system that is unwieldy, slow, and directed more towards preserving precedent than creating productive solutions for the parties. This is the state of affairs that we all take for granted. We assume it is the only viable course of action. We have stopped asking ourselves whether the current state of affairs is acceptable to us. The whole system is essentially invisible to everyone involved. Eliminating blind spots starts with questioning the obvious.

Safety and Power

The meaning of the term "safety"—like the meaning of the terms "truth" and "justice"—is difficult to condense into a universally useful definition. The meaning of safety is unavoidably subjective, and experience teaches us that safety cannot be guaranteed. Nevertheless, it is worth giving the matter careful attention because it is the role of the contract and contract law to provide as much safety as possible in support of creative, productive co-venturing.

To optimize the effectiveness of contracts, we need to know what "safety" a contract is supposed to provide. In other words, in the context of a business contractual relationship, *what do the parties need* in order to be confident it is safe for them to move forward?

Parties want to know they have a foundational platform for their venture that they can put their weight on—that will support and sustain the success of their venture. They need sufficient predictability to enable them to plan effectively. They want to feel confident that they can rely on one another to live up to promises and obligations, and they want assurance that they each will have the power to protect and preserve their own well-being and the beneficial purpose of their bargain. In sum, in the context of a contractual relationship, I find that it is useful to define "safety" as *having sufficient predictability, so that the parties' expectations are reasonably assured, enabling them to plan and venture with well-founded confidence that each will retain the power to take a meaningful role in responding to changing circumstances and will have an equal voice and be treated fairly should conflict arise.*

Taking Back the Power

An axiom of contract law is that the contract is the parties' "private law." The idea is that parties should have the power to design their ideal business relationships and ventures by establishing their own, customized system for clarity and certainty. The government enables private parties to write their own private law by agreeing to enforce the terms and conditions of their contracts because, theoretically, this encourages creativity and enterprise to the benefit of all of society. So long as it does not conflict with laws of the larger system or public policy, the proprietary system that the parties create, as described in their written contract, will be enforced.

We lawyers sometimes forget, and nonlawyers are often not aware, how much leeway the parties have to design their own *legal systems* using this private law embodied by the contract.

Typically, we pull out the last couple of contracts we negotiated for similar deals (contracts that were based on antecedent versions of other past deals backwards through time unfathomed), and we begin revising. It is a rare contract that includes a structure that supports the parties in retaining the power to craft their own real-time responses to disruptive change, crisis, and disagreement and also provides a creative regenerative way, rather than a destructive way, to do so.

Alternative Approach—Sense and Respond

No one can know or control what will happen in the future as a consequence of any given action or decision. Each transaction, every business endeavor, is a conversation, a cocreation with other actors—coparties, forces of politics, marketplace dynamics, and the caprices of nature. Interdependence is a fact, whether we acknowledge it or not. Individual well-being is inextricably linked to the intentions, actions, and well-being of others. Every relationship is an ongoing conversation, and traditional contracts provide only a snapshot of one static point in the dynamic exchange.

Serious reflection on the contradiction between our belief in control and our experience of uncertainty reveal that the conventional "predict and control" approach is not optimal in today's dynamic, disruptive marketplace. The inadequacies of the existing system challenge us to consider the possibility of creating a better system, one that the parties themselves can use to notice, explore, and resolve tensions that arise between them in the course of their transaction or endeavor.

It can be hard to trust that such a thing is possible in the context of a contractual dispute. The adversarial, coercive paradigm is so ingrained in our thinking we believe it is inevitable that conflict generates combat, and that combat can be resolved only within a hierarchical framework where some outside entity has the power to impose a resolution. But we've all experienced the reality of the "pyrrhic" victory and the sad destruction of what should have been beneficial relationships.

The way to escape the trap is to never enter it, to change who the "decider" will be and shift the parties from adversaries to cooperative problem solvers.

From Swords to Ploughshares

Yes, there are disputes that should be in the courts, but not every dispute, not even most disputes need to be litigated—especially not those disputes that have arisen from disagreements between coparties who originally intended to work in harmony to their mutual benefit. What's needed are structures and systems that will direct energy and effort toward solving the underlying problems that have given rise to the conflict and will put the power in the hands of those best qualified to understand and grapple with the complexity of context and circumstance—the parties themselves.

What can we do to enable the parties to function and even thrive in the midst of disruption and uncertainty?

We can help the parties establish a firm foundation for a productive, resilient relationship. Rather than blindly accepting the existing system and its underlying logic, the formation of the contract becomes a moment of conscious choice. Instead of using the contract as a weapon of war, the parties use it to design and build a proprietary system for addressing change and engaging conflict that gives them a way to harness the creative potential inherent in conflict.

In addition to plotting their plan of action and settling their deal points, the parties can use the negotiation conversation to calibrate the appropriateness and the trustworthiness of the proposed relationship. The contract document becomes a handbook they use to maintain and—if needed—restore the trust necessary for a productive, successful, sustainable relationship.

This possibility is not as remote or revolutionary as one might imagine. The traditional practice of law is already expanding to embrace collaborative approaches, systems, and structures; examples of cocreative responses to the challenges of the modern marketplace are legion. In fact, the business world is leading the way in changing the perception that top-down, hierarchical structures are optimal for success. New operating assumptions and operational logics are being tested and proven on the radically challenging, digital, networked frontier.[2]

With the advent of the Internet, a new transparency has brought awareness of our global interconnectedness and interdependence. Expectations about the role of business in society are changing. Emerging leaders believe business should be a force for good in the world (defining "good" far more broadly than mere shareholder ROI[3]) and that business answers to an authority and obligation of greater scope than regulations, statutes, and legal compliance. Double and triple bottom lines that address societal and environmental impacts have become accepted measures of success.[4]

Designing contracts that recognize and address the greater good— for society and for the parties' own relationship—is not

---

[2] Robertson, Brian J. *Holacracy: The New Management System for a Rapidly Changing World.* Henry Holt, 2015. Print.; Denning, Steve. "Making Sense of Zappos and Holacracy." *Forbes.* Forbes Magazine, 15 Jan. 2014. Web. 27 Aug. 2015.; "What Is the Difference Between a Benefit Corporation and a B Corp? – Cutting Edge Capital." *Cutting Edge Capital.* 28May 2013. Web. 27 Aug. 2015.

[3] Return On Investment.

[4] "Triple Bottom Line." *The Economist.* The Economist Newspaper, 17 Nov. 2009. Web. 27 Aug. 2015. (article adapted from "The Economist Guide to Management Ideas and Gurus," Hindle, Tim. London: Profile, 2008. Print.); *see generally,* "TriplePundit: Reporting on the Triple Bottom Line & Sustainable Business News." *Triple Pundit People Planet Profit.* Triple Pundit, LLC., n.d. Web. 27 Aug. 2015.

just forward thinking, it is vital for the practice of law in the new reality of digital-speed, globally connected communities and enterprises.

CHAPTER 2

Evolving Business
Realities and Mindsets

We shape our tools, and thereafter our tools shape us.
—Marshall McLuhan

In the time since the World Wide Web and the "information super highway" first registered in public awareness, the impact on commerce has been surprisingly swift and completely transformative. The pervasiveness of the Internet is now taken for granted. It is hard to recall a time before instantaneous communication and abundant information, yet it is only in the last 20 years that widespread use of the Internet has taken off.

Accessibility of information has exploded. News used to be delivered to our homes morning and evening by the paperboy or TV news anchors. Now, information about events in far-flung corners of the earth, as well as local happenings, is fed in a constant stream to devices we carry everywhere and check with increasing obsession. What is more, individual commentary and contribution to the flow of information are distributed globally at the same digital speed and scale. We, as individuals, can now participate in a global, real-time conversation.

Even *things* are now interconnected. Objects we never think of as communications devices send signals via wireless networks. Physical products are no longer just whiz-bang gizmos we love to own and use, they are portals to networked services. Products come embedded with technology that allows them to send information back to the manufacturer about our use habits and the functionality of the item itself. Consumers are coming to understand that when they use a device, even those as mundane and personal as a coffeemaker or automobile, they are contributing information to a remote database. And in return, they expect to receive personalized services and problem solving. As customers become active agents of product evolution, the line between producers and consumers is blurred. Consumers are becoming "prosumers"[1] collaborating with one another and, via these collaborative communities, participating in product development.

These tectonic shifts in communications are generating new ways of interacting—as humans and as participants in the world economy, business, and society. The new post-Internet reality is an interconnected, democratized, radically transparent and networked social and business culture. This new world challenges our presumptions about organization of society, business, autonomy, and power; and the evolving culture demands change in the operational assumptions and logic of social and legal systems and structures.

Changing the Locus of Control

The emerging networked society and marketplace do not presume a linear flow to and from a centralized seat of control. New decentralized models of collaboration are developing, enabled by the combination of peer-to-peer information sharing, social media and pervasive computing (a.k.a. "the Internet of Things").[2]

---

[1] Rifkin, Jeremy. "Chapter Nine: The Ascent of the Prosumer and the Build-out of the Smart Economy." *The Zero Marginal Cost Society: The Internet of Things, the Collaborative Commons, and the Eclipse of Capitalism.* New York: Palgrave/Macmillan, 2014. 135–51. Print.

[2] *The Internet of Things Meets the Internet of People Infinite Interactions Drives New Values.* Harbor Research, 2010. PDF.

As the threshold to enter the mass-communications arena has lowered, control over content and message also has been democratized. Consequently, the content streaming across the network has become less standardized than when it was fed only through portals controlled by individual companies or governments. With use of social media increasing exponentially, the ability to influence public opinion and harness public willpower is no longer in the hands of an elite few. Formerly disparate, individual voices are finding one another and forming communities of affinity. Because we are more connected, collaborative, participatory, visible, and accountable, it is easier to observe and comprehend interdependence and the mutuality of the well-being of those we might otherwise see as separate individuals/communities.

Social media favors self-organized groups and efforts over top-down organizations. Examples of horizontal distribution of voice and power, organized on-the-fly by participants and wielded via social media are myriad. They include the events of the so-called Arab Spring, nationwide demonstrations in the United States triggered by the viral spread of citizen videos showing local police activities, the quick-time revision of its "Religious Freedom" statute by Indiana's legislature in response to nationwide outrage expressed online,[3] and the astonishing efficacy of calls for financial assistance posted via the "Humans of New York" Facebook page with its more than 18 million readers,[4] to name just a few.

Networked self-organization also means those immediately affected by a particular situation can collaborate to codesign solutions in real-time, addressing specific needs and obstacles in ways that serve their unique circumstances. For example, in the aftermath of Hurricane Sandy, the affected communities did not

---

[3] Montanaro, Dominico. "Indiana Law: Sorting Fact from Fiction from Politics." *NPR*. NPR, 1 Apr. 2015. Web. 25 Aug. 2015

[4] Johnson, M. Alex. "Humans of New York Raises $2 Million to End Forced Labor in Pakistan." *NBC News*. 19 Aug. 2015. Web. 25 Aug. 2015.

wait for FEMA but turned immediately to Facebook and other social media portals to more precisely target need with direct assistance, playing a crucial role in disaster response and ongoing recovery efforts.[5] Individuals self-organizing to engage and manage the context, complexity, and uniqueness of their own particular circumstances and to aggregate their voices across nations and continents to trigger change, translates into the ultimate expression of We The People living empowered, immediate, and democratically self-determined lives.

Networks, Not Silos

In the business arena as well, the efficacy of traditional hierarchical structures is being challenged. New entrepreneurial communities are participatory and collaborative, with foundational principles such as "fail fast, learn, evolve."[6] Thomas Edison famously said, "I have not failed. I've just found 10,000 ways that don't work." The image of the lonely inventor toiling away for years in his lab until he makes the get-rich breakthrough is fading as innovation becomes an open-source collaboration amongst a global, voluntarily affiliated community of participants. Many hands make lighter (and faster) work. Capabilities, risks, and rewards are distributed across a network, and complex projects are completed ever more rapidly by peer producers.[7] By allowing independent programmers free access to

---

[5] Gilbert, Alison. "Social Media and Hurricane Sandy." *Digital Ethos.* 15 Nov. 2012. Web. 25 Aug. 2015; "Social Media and Hurricanes What We've Learned Since Sandy." *Social Media and Hurricanes What We've Learned Since Sandy.* Homeland Security Science and Technology, n.d. Web. 25 Aug. 2015.

[6] "Agile Methodology Understanding Agile Methodology." *Agile Methodology RSS.* Web. 25 Aug. 2015.; McGrath, Rita. "Failing by Design." *Harvard Business Review.* 01 Apr. 2011. Web. 25 Aug. 2015.

[7] Zhu, Dengya, Vidyasagar Potdar, and Elizabeth Chang. "Open Source Software Development (OSSD) Based On Software Engineering." *IFIP International Federation for Information Processing Open Source Systems* (2006): 345–46. Web. 25 Aug. 2015.

and use of the code necessary to design new apps for Apple devices, the desirability, functionality, and marketplace success of those devices has been exponentially increased—far beyond what might have been possible if Apple more tightly managed use of the software platform.[8] This free-wheeling, improvisational approach to marketplace relation ships and cooperative effort can confound traditional legal assumptions about ownership and affiliation, and relentlessly presents novel questions about how the constantly morphing collaborative undertaking should or could interface with the existing legal system and body of laws.

The organizational logic—that self-interest can be better served by collaborative effort and sharing of resources—is not a new concept in thought or practice. It is the logic of the commons and is as old as the human community.[9] The Internet is a vast commons, an interactive participatory arena that, in turn, is used to generate and support multiple other commons-based endeavors—collaborative arrangements in which access is often more important than ownership.[10] In contrast to conventional hierarchical structures, the modern commons has a different set of operating assumptions, and alternative organizational structures apply, all serving an alternative definition of success.

---

[8] "Apple Open Source." *Apple Open Source.* Web. 25 Aug. 2015. <http://www.apple.com/opensource/>.

[9] Wall, Derek. *The Commons in History: Culture, Conflict, and Ecology.* MIT, 2014. Print.; Rifkin, Jeremy. "Chapter One: The Great Paradigm Shift from Market Capitalism to the Collaborative Commons." *The Zero Marginal Cost Society: The Internet of Things, the Collaborative Commons, and the Eclipse of Capitalism.* New York: Palgrave/Macmillan, 2014. 1–25. Print.

[10] "The logic of the [Internet] is to optimize lateral peer production, universal access, and inclusion, the same sensibilities that are critical to the nurturing and creation of social capital in the civil society. The very purpose of the new technology platform is to encourage a sharing culture, which is what the Commons is all about. It is these design features of the Internet of Things that bring the social Commons out of the shadows, giving it a high-tech platform to become the dominant economic paradigm of the twenty-first century." Rifkin, *supra* p.18.

The logic of the commons sees success not so much as a finish line crossed than as a quality of sustainability of mutual benefits and well-being.[11]

As demonstrated by the transformational impact of social media, of peer-to-peer, open-source development, and crowd-sourcing models, the new post-Internet commons derives from collaborative systems intentionally designed, organized, and maintained by and for all of its constituents, grounded in the purpose of cocreating and sustaining wealth (as the community defines it) for everyone.

Today's emerging business leaders and innovators came of age in a world where the Internet with all its reach and pervasiveness was already the norm. They've grown up in a networked world where every voice is heard and every individual can participate. They play massive multiplayer games; they are constantly in touch with a global community; and they use social media to harness that community, aggregating and asserting influence. Interdependence, collaborative production, collaborative consumption, and horizontal, self-organizing structures are intuitive to this new wave of entrepreneurs.

Not trapped by the fly-paper stickiness of conventional models and mindsets, members of the "Millennial Generation" of entrepreneurs are conceiving and testing new ways to organize group efforts and maintain the sort of communal harmony that supports the abiding and trustworthy relationships crucial to the success of collaborative endeavors. They are rethinking business practices and demonstrating the economic power and financial rewards of open collaboration and crowd-sourced innovation. Simple truths, such as the importance of exclusive control of intellectual property rights, are no longer either simple or true.

---

[11] "Markets are beginning to give way to networks, ownership is becoming less important than access, the pursuit of self-interest is being tempered by the pull of collaborative interests, and the traditional dream of rags to riches is being supplanted by a new dream of a sustainable quality of life." Rifkin, p.523.

For this generation, the interconnectedness of the well-being of all creatures is not just a philosophical concept; it is a visceral experience. The real-time delivery of information combined with the new, distributed ability to impact events—to frame the story, to influence popular opinion, and to generate mass action—has taught them that isolation is a delusion and the well-being of the individual and the "tribe" is inextricably entangled with the actions and well-being of all others.

Collaborative Wealth and Success

New Republic senior editor Gregg Easterbrook has observed, 'A transition from material want to meaning want is in progress on an historically unprecedented scale—involving hundreds of millions of people—and may eventually be recognized as the principle cultural development of our age.
   —*Rajendra Sisodia, David B. Wolfe, and Jagdish N. Sheth. Firms of Endearment: How World-Class Companies Profit from Passion and Purpose.*

A new way of defining "wealth" is emerging from the experiences of the dynamic and collaborative realities of the 21st-century marketplace. Relationships, trust, adaptability, sustainability, and access to (rather than ownership of) resources are among the new keystones of success.

The growing collaborative commons brings a new understanding of "power" beyond the top-down ability to coerce others' compliance by enforcing rights or compelling performance. This, in turn, leads to a reexamination of the idea that "safety" is reliably grounded in traditional concepts of success, wealth, and power. Successful business and leadership are increasingly identified with words like "consciousness"[12] and "meaning" in addition to market share and return on investment (ROI).[13]

Consumers are participating with companies beyond the merely transactional customer/provider relationship. The ongoing, postpurchase personalization of the product and experience heightens the sense of a *personal* relationship between the consumer and the provider. Through the interactive, collaborative conversation companies become ever more visible members of their customers' communities. The viral nature of social media means that consumers are actively holding companies accountable for the quality of corporate citizenship. How well the company understands and follows through on this implicit relationship and community membership can affect the goodwill associated with the company's reputation and, by extension, the company's fiscal health.

Customers are more aware and informed than ever before, and they are making choices based on their informed awareness. In deciding whether to purchase, customers respond to more than the "what" (the product or service offered), looking also to the "why" (what it means to support a company by buying its products/services). By raising their networked voices through social media and by voting with their Dollars, Euro, Bitcoin, etc., individuals are taking responsibility for their own role in how business impacts social and environmental factors.

According to Nielsen's "Global Survey on Corporate

---

[12] Kofman, Fred. *Conscious Business: How to Build Value through Values.* Boulder, CO: Sounds True, 2006. Print.; Sisodia, Rajendra, Jagdish N. Sheth, and David B. Wolfe. *Firms of Endearment: How World-class Companies Profit from Passion and Purpose.* 2nd ed. Pearson Education, 2014. Print.; Schwartz, Tony. "Companies That Practice 'Conscious Capitalism' Perform 10x Better." *Harvard Business Review.* 04 Apr. 2013. Web. 25 Aug. 2015.; Zender, Tom. "Discover the Power of Consciousness in Your Business Phoenix Business Journal." *Phoenix Business Journal.* N.p., 2 Jan. 2015. Web. 25 Aug. 2015
[13] Sinek, Simon. *Start with Why: How Great Leaders Inspire Everyone to Take Action.* New York: Portfolio, 2009. Print.

*Social Responsibility," 43% of global consumers said
they are willing to spend more for a product or service
that supports a cause.*

—*Jeff King and Jeff Fromm*[14]

In the modern collaborative commons, the conversation is
changing from "who owns what," to "who are we and how do
we treat one an-. other," and to "what connects us and how are
we impacting our mutual and respective well-being."
Stewardship and abiding, trustworthy relationships increase in
value compared with ownership of private capital and discrete,
impersonal transactions.

Conscience and Consciousness

*This new universe of social activity is being built on
the foundation of a very different ethics and social
logic than that of homo economics—the economist's
fiction that we are all selfish, utility-maximizing,
rational materialists.*

—*David Bollier*[15]

"Consciousness" has entered the business vernacular. The word
is generally used to describe a values-based way of doing
business, intentionally serving some identified purpose other
than (and in addition to) financial ROI. Most often, it seems to
be a moniker applied to companies that declare an intent to serve
a "triple bottom line" comprising financial, social, and
environmental imperatives. Using the word in this way

---

[14] King, Jeff, and Jeff Fromm. "Only Conscious Capitalists Will Survive."
Forbes. Forbes Magazine, 4 Dec. 2013. Web. 24 Aug. 2015

[15] "The New Economic Events Giving Lie to the Fiction That We Are All
Selfish, Rational Materialists." *Alternet*. Independent Media Institute, 14 Apr.
2014. Web. 24 Aug. 2015.

encourages a tendency to conflate "consciousness" with "conscience." It is important, however, to distinguish between the two. Conscience is a subjective sense of rightness or wrongness. Consciousness is "a capacity to be aware and to choose."[16]

Having one does not necessitate exercising the other. One can have a conscience and not be acting consciously in its service, and one can operate consciously yet be completely devoid of conscience. Knowing the content of one's conscience falls within the "awareness" aspect of consciousness, and intentional decision making in accordance with conscience is the "choosing" element. Ben & Jerry's is a familiar example of a business that embodied both having a conscience (a moral and ethical code), and also being conscious (aware of the contents of the conscience and making choices accordingly).[17] Researchers are discovering that so-called "conscious" businesses, those which make relational capital a top priority by valuing and honoring the needs of all their stakeholders (not solely the shareholders), are reliably outperforming companies that maintain the conventional focus on a financial-returns-only bottom line.[18]

When Worlds Collide

Our Age of Anxiety is, in great part, the result of trying to do today's jobs with yesterday's tools!

—Marshall McLuhan

---

[16] Kofman, Fred. *Conscious Business*. Rec. 1 Sept. 2006. Sounds True, 2006. CD.

[17] *Biography: Ben and Jerry*. By Amy Martinez. Perf. Liz Bankowski, Ben Cohen, Zak Fine. 2006. TV Episode.

[18] Schwartz, Tony. "Companies That Practice 'Conscious Capitalism' Perform 10x Better." *Harvard Business Review*. 04 Apr. 2013. Web. 25 Aug. 2015.; Berfield, Susan. "Container Store: Conscious Capitalism and the Perils of Going Public." *Bloomberg.com*. Bloomberg Businessweek, 19 Feb. 2015. Web. 24 Aug. 2015.

Since the advent of the Internet, there have been ongoing attempts to reconcile capitalism's self-interested/material-gain focus with this new global technological platform uniquely designed to facilitate and encourage sharing, collaboration, and decentralization of power and influence. When use of the Internet first began to accelerate, conversations about ownership and protection of "intellectual property" ("IP") were at the forefront, and in short order there were profound challenges to meet. Napster's peer-to-peer sharing software sent shockwaves throughout the music industry and beyond, creating confusion and dissent in both the business and legal arenas. The Napster software was one of the first examples of "disruptive" Internet technology, fundamentally and almost instantaneously changing the way the market worked, laying explosive charges under the pillars upon which capitalism and its supporting legal system were constructed. There has followed a deluge of disruption. Notable examples abound including Netflix, Huffington Post, and Airbnb, among many others. Long-standing business truths, along with structures and systems based on them, are being called into question. Vertical, hierarchical operating principles are giving way to ideas that seem ill-advised to pre-Internet sensibilities and for which the legal system was ill-prepared.[19]

The logic on which conventional systems are based, arose from and perpetuates the conventional mindsets about how success is created and how business flourishes. Our legacy framework for organizing business and law is hierarchical. The idea of open-source innovation is profoundly counterintuitive to many business people and lawyers who are accustomed to achieving and sustaining competitive dominance and the "return

---

[19] Anders, George. "Gurus Gone Wild: Does Zappos' Reorganization Make Any Sense?" Forbes. Forbes Magazine, 9 Jan. 2014.; "The Holes in Holacracy." *The Economist*. The Economist Newspaper, 05 July 2014.; "Yes, You Can Make Money with Open Source." *Harvard Business Review*. 15 Jan. 2013.; Boldren, Michele, and David K. Levine. "Open-Source Software: Who Needs Intellectual Property? | Foundation for Economic Education." *FEE Freeman Article*. Foundation for Economic Education, 1 Jan. 2007.

on investment" goals of conventional capitalist models by creating and fiercely protecting proprietary rights. It is unimaginable that sharing resources, products, and services for free could translate into the profits required by conventional models. It seems a lunatic proposition.

But business, indeed society as a whole, is conducted in a profoundly different environment than in pre-Internet days. Companies are having to reconceive what it means to be stable and well-managed, while legal counsel must wrestle with the application of conventional legal concepts and structures across this new frontier.[20]

Law "as usual" is no longer a viable option. When business is conducted at digital-speed, conventional approaches and practices, including those regarding contract formation, drafting, and enforcement, are often too slow. Contract negotiations focused on predicting every potential pitfall and then drafting provisions to control the imagined future are woefully inadequate in a world where disruption can make nonsense of the most carefully crafted plan. The "four corners" of the document cannot encompass fast-paced, ever-evolving marketplace realities. Deal-making and project launches cannot wait for glacial-speed negotiation and drafting. In many instances, the parties begin performance before the deal points have been fully explored (much less formally agreed). They move forward assuring themselves and one another that they will be able to hammer out any issues as they arise. If a dispute between the parties does arise, the lumbering pace of legal processes and proceedings creates an unacceptable drag on the agility required to compete in a marketplace where change and disruption are almost routine. Business cannot wait for the staid and sluggish pace of the legal system. Business has to respond in real-time,

---

[20] Wall, Matthew. "Innovate or Die: The Stark Message for Big Business BBC News." *BBC News*. BBC News Services, 5 Sept. 2014. Web. 27 Aug. 2015.; Satell, Greg. "Managing For Disruption." *Forbes*. Forbes Magazine, 13 Mar. 2014. Web. 27 Aug. 2015.

immediately and effectively.

What is more, with instant connection and high visibility, the digital-speed distribution of networked information means the whole world is a glass fishbowl. Transparency, long considered an undesirable vulnerability, is now virtually inevitable. In days not long gone, lawyers routinely advised clients to consider how the correspondence they were about to send would reflect on them if it were published on the front page of the local paper. Today, the question is, "How would this look if it went viral?"

The new transparency brought about by social media means that old-style tactics have to be rethought and revised. Object lessons abound. United Airlines had a customer relations nightmare when an unhappy passenger created the now famous video, "United Breaks Guitars." The song has generated a new career for the singer-songwriter who memorialized his experience in a music video.[21] When the Susan Komen Foundation sent out conventional cease-and-desist letters in an attempt to enforce exclusive rights to use "FOR THE CURE," public outcry was swift and harsh. Articles ran in the *Wall Street Journal* and *Huffington Post* highlighting stories of small, sparsely funded nonprofits facing what was characterized as trademark bullying.[22] By contrast, a letter from Jack Daniels' lawyer was widely praised for its politeness and genteel approach. Their "nicest cease-and-desist order of all time" became a nationwide exemplar for taking a stand without using intimidation tactics.[23]

---

[21] How Saving $1200 Cost United Airlines 10,772,839 Negative Views on YouTube—http://sentium. com/a-public-relations-disaster-how-saving-1200 -cost-united-airlines-10772839-negative-views-on youtube/; www.youtube.com/watch?v=5YGc4zOqozo

[22] "Susan Komen Foundation Elbows Out Charities Over Use of the Word "Cure"—http://www. huffingtonpost.com/2010/12/07/komen-foundation -charities-cure_n_793176.html; "Charity Brawl: Nonprofits Aren't So Generous When a Name's at Stake"—*Wall Street Journal*—http://www.wsj.com/ articles/SB10001424052748703700904575390950178142586.

[23] "Jack Daniels Wrote What Has To Be The Nicest Cease-And-Desist Order

As these examples demonstrate, approaches to disputes that have been effective in the past and are appropriate from the perspective of the legal system, now can generate a toxic level of backlash that does more damage than the good such efforts were meant to achieve. The sense of community membership, the democratization of voice and influence, the reality of interconnectedness and interdependence, have changed the equation for handling disruptive change and conflict.

Legal responses to business needs must enter the 21st century. Lawyers need to be able to offer clients strategies that support agility and resilience in a dynamic marketplace while also affording adequate safety to protect companies' interests without harming companies' relational capital. The time has come for legal thinking, practices, and systems to join the stream of progress, to shift to conscious awareness of how legal actions and attitudes impact the speed, agility, and relational capital that is key to business success in this brave new world.

The fates lead him who will; him who won't, they drag.
—Lucius Annaeus Seneca (4 BC–65 AD)

Of All Time"—http:// all-time-2012-7; "Jack Daniels' Cease-and-Desist Letter Goes Viral for Being Exceedingly Polite"—http://www.abajournal.com/news/article/jack_daniels_cease-and-desist_letter_goes_viral_for_being_exceeedingly_poli/

CHAPTER 3

Cause of Action

Adapting the legal system to the evolving needs of 21st-century business is a task that seems daunting at best and utterly impossible at worst. How can an overburdened and lumbering legal system have any hope of keeping up with the quicksilver, digital-speed marketplace? How can law, which must be debated, codified, correlated, and seemingly chiseled in stone, provide adequate protection for businesses engaging in intentional, virtually instantaneous, and constant change?

> *No doubt the ideal system, if it were attainable, would be a code at once so flexible and so minute, as to supply in advance for every conceivable situation the just and fitting rule. But life is too complex to bring the attainment of this ideal within the compass of human powers.*
>
> *—Benjamin Nathan Cardozo,*
> *The Nature of the Judicial Process (1921).*

It is not possible to create a set of rules and responses that will prove *fitting and just* for every eventuality; and rules alone cannot provide a structure *flexible and minute* enough to serve the specific needs of particular parties, as those needs arise in the midst of complex and ever-shifting business realities.

Contract language is often used to define *desired behavior* and includes incentives for exhibiting the behavior and penalties for failing to do so, while other contract provisions take the opposite approach. Rather than defining and incentivizing desired behaviors, these provisions focus on preventing something from happening—breach, loss, delay. Unfortunately, it is not unusual for rules, incentives, and penalties included in a contract to end up creating more problems than they prevent.

Incentives, rules, and penalties influence behavior by putting focus on collecting the incentive and avoiding penalties rather than on doing what makes sense in the actual situation. They can also create pressures that make literal interpretations of the rules and incentives (following the "letter of the law") a more attractive option than doing the right thing. For example, health care business agreements that reward doctors based on the number of patients seen within a given time can discourage the measured pace and careful listening crucial to proper diagnosis and treatment, and can also discourage doctors from getting adequate rest. The promotion and pay structures in Big Law—often linked to billable hour requirements and bonus thresholds—can create tension for associates and paralegals between what is best for the client (working efficiently and quickly) and what seems good for the associate's career and financial outlook (logging a high number of billable hours). These tensions can lead some associates and paralegals to hide work from others or continue working when physically and mentally exhausted; and a few succumb to the temptation to "pad" their time-keeping records in favor of higher billables.[1]

The parties to a contract focus on exhibiting the desired behaviors in order to achieve the contractual rewards and avoid the contractual sanctions, regardless of whether those behaviors make sense or are beneficial to the endeavor. The behaviors, while looking good on paper at the time the contract was written, have unintended consequences and can turn out not to be what is actually needed in the face of the real-life situations that arise in

---

[1] "Law Firm Hours – The Real Story." *Above the Law*. Lateral Link, 24 July 2012. Web. 27 Aug. 2015.; see generally, Schwartz, Barry, and Kenneth Sharpe. *Practical Wisdom: The Right Way to Do the Right Thing*. 1st ed. New York: Riverhead, 2010. Print.

the course of doing business. But because those behaviors have been codified in the contract, the humans involved repeat the behaviors over and over. Thus, the contract itself functions as a sort of silent partner—to whom all parties are held accountable, a partner who must be appeased, and who becomes the ultimate definer of success and dispenser of rewards. The parties no longer feel free to do what makes sense for the endeavor but are instead bound by rules that are often obsolete before the printer paper cools.

Typically, we write contracts to try and create certainty—making assumptions about a stable, knowable world in which our contract terms will make us safe. Certainty equates to answers. We pose hypotheticals and then put solutions in place to manage those imagined scenarios, leaving little room for future adaptability or flexibility in light of evolving circumstances or the complexity of actual context. The truth is, things are certain to change. When conflict arises, the contractual rules, incentives, and penalties turn the parties' attention to the past. They must look backward and channel energy and attention into assigning blame, fault, loss, and punishment, away from steering the best course forward in the new climate and landscape. It is an impossible way to navigate.

No sailor imagines that it is possible or wise set a course then sail in strict compliance without allowing for weather, waves, and the paths of other vessels. We don't sail successfully to a destination by trying to prevent ourselves from arriving elsewhere or by arguing about which choices shouldn't have been made in the past. Sailors plot a course based on the intended destination, set the heading, and then start the journey— navigating by known markers and responding to what happens along the way. Everyone understands that course corrections will be necessary and inevitable in crossing the seas of uncertainty. Course corrections are not "breaches" of the plan.

Incentives, rules, and penalties are often an obstacle to making the inevitable course corrections needed to successfully navigate the waters of business today. Safety, we must remember, is about *sufficient predictability*, not concrete, predetermined certainty. It is about having reasonably assured expectations and retaining the power to take a meaningful role in responding to changing circumstances.

> *Rules make things complicated, they subvert the parties' ability to act on 'common sense,' on intuition, on experience...with creativity.*
>
> —*Philip K. Howard*[2]

Even defining certain behaviors as good or bad is not sufficient. The context within which an action is taken and the perspective from which it is judged will radically change whether that action is perceived as "good" or "bad." We need a way to evaluate a proposed action or plan that is not solely dependent on rules, incentives, or penalties. We need to know how to determine what makes sense—what the criteria are for staying on course while allowing for the flexibility needed to adapt within a dynamic, digital-speed marketplace.

When a business relationship is created and governed by contract, how do the parties build a kind of "sense and respond" agility into that document? Can they? Or must they draft addendums ad infinitum? Or worse, just ignore the contract terms and gamble that they won't ever find themselves in a situation where obsolete provisions are applied to a complex reality that no longer matches the landscape in which the original agreement was struck?

What we need is a navigational heading that provides the lodestar by which the journey is undertaken—allowing for course corrections, tacking when needed—with the ability to determine whether the venturers are off course, how far, and how to best get back on course.

---

[2] Howard, Phillip K. "Four Ways to Fix a Broken Legal System." *Philip K. Howard:*. TED, Feb. 2010. Web. 24 Aug. 2015.

Rather than imagining the future and drafting contract terms to address all possible scenarios, it makes far more sense to use the contract to establish a system for dealing with the inevitable uncertainties the parties will face. We must change our approach, so they can sail forward with confidence that parties can adapt and change course *as a team* with the assurance that they are working in tandem and not at cross-purposes.

The Place to Start

To do this, we must dig deeper. Although rules and incentives certainly exert pressures on behaviors and choices, ultimately what really drive us are our intrinsic values, core interests, and needs. These basic values and needs drive our actions far more directly than any contractual obligation.

For most parties, the contract document is something that belongs more to the legal professionals than to the business people. Business people sign and date the document, then send it to the file and immediately begin operating in a way that makes intuitive sense to them. This can be fine, so long as the parties' respective intuitive, common sense responses to challenges are aligned. If their underlying motivations and needs are not aligned, however, the wheels can come off the wagon rather quickly. What makes perfect sense to one can appear lunatic or even malicious to the other. What is even more unfortunate is that each party involved is shocked and surprised and feels as if the other party is being intentionally aggressive in undermining the endeavor.

The parties take actions to serve real needs and interests. They parse contractual language to rationalize or justify the actions. The argument over whether the contract can be understood to support a given action misdirects attention to interpreting language and away from serving the underlying needs and interests that gave rise to the controversial actions.

It is far better to identify potentially opposing motivations and needs before the contract is signed. It is ultimately more efficient and realistic to get to the heart of what really drives the parties—and express that as clearly and completely as possible— during the contract drafting rather than later when faced with a crisis that may not fit the incentives and penalties laid out in a conventional, predictive document.

Interests and needs that are not compatible can be discussed in the incubation of the project and reconciled in a nonthreatening, far less emotionally charged environment. Differences can be discussed and the relative importance of various motivations and needs can be understood before the contract is ever signed. If motivations and needs are clearly understood and defined in advance, the parties have a basis for knowing how to address unexpected future crises in a way that will be mutually acceptable and even—dare we dream— mutually beneficial.

Once motivations and needs are determined to be in alignment, the contract must still provide a way for the parties to make boots-on-the-ground decisions that continue to align with the declared motivations. Aligned responsiveness is far safer than compelled adherence to what we hope are stable, accurate predictions. Rules can be useful to set the boundaries of the field of freedom and autonomy of the parties— what must and what must not be done—but it is the clarity, alignment, and explicit expression of the parties' motivations and needs that orient and guide the actions taken within these boundaries and that support cocreative decision making when the boundaries themselves no longer make sense.

Head in the Sand Contracts

And yet these basic motivational drivers are rarely, if ever, examined during the contract formation process. In fact, the parties themselves may not be fully aware of what is driving their own decisions. They generally have a sense of what feels right, fair, or wise, but rarely have they articulated—even for themselves—what is at the root of their impulse/intuition. Unexpressed motivations and values still motivate and drive decisions. It is quite easy for potential business partners to have incompatible motivations for doing the project or incompatible values around how to do the project without realizing it until well after the contract is signed and the project is underway.[3] During the contract negotiation and drafting period, attention is channeled towards how to make the rules work rather than how the parties will understand and do what's best for everyone in a particular situation.

A trustworthy, safe contractual relationship is one in which the parties can plan and venture with confidence that they retain the power to take a meaningful role in responding to change and will be treated fairly should conflict arise. Establishing such a contractual relationship begins with an intentional exploration and expression of the parties' motivations, needs, values, and decision drivers. Safety and trust are built by bringing these into focus and calibrating alignment.

Conventional contract provisions attend to clarifying and aligning the transactional aspects of the business relationship. Alignment of goals and roles is certainly important to a smooth transaction or venture, but is not enough. Beyond purely transactional alignment, a resilient, sustainable relationship is grounded in alignment of the deeper motivations of the parties. Exploring and expressing core values, vision, and principles forms the basis for a lasting, mutually beneficial relationship and

---

[3] "We truly believed that Costanoa had a great long-term future ahead of it. It's just that we had a different definition of success than our investors. And this lack of transactional alignment was starting to affect our mutual trust in each other...Now each time we engage in a potential new hotel project, we have a series of key questions we ask the primary investor group (if we aren't raising the money ourselves) to ensure that we have alignment regarding the transaction." Conley, Chip. "Chapter Ten: Creating Trust." *Peak: How Great Companies Get Their Mojo from Maslow*. 1st ed. San Francisco: Jossey-Bass, 2007. p.174. Print.

sets the stage for success.

But how do we do this? We are lawyers, not psychologists.

It's not as hard as it may sound. We do it by framing.

Importance of Frame

The way a photographer frames an image determines the relative importance of the various objects in the photo. In setting the frame, the photographer chooses the context that influences how we interpret the meaning of the image. The frame determines the boundaries of what we see. Frames choose what is included and what is excluded from consideration, and frames orient us— choosing our focal points and establishing a perspective that impacts how we understand the relationships between everything that falls within the frame.

> *Frames tell us what is important and help us establish what should be compared with what. [They help us] discern what is relevant about a particular context or event in regard to the decision we face.*
>
> —*Barry Schwartz*[4]

Lawyers are advised to frame their argument, frame the issue; but what about the frames we carry with us without conscious awareness? What about the cultural assumptions that form the frame for our evaluation of right, wrong, powerful, weak, winning, and losing?

Social institutions (like systems of laws and adjudication) are created in response to cultural beliefs. Transformation of social institutions must begin with examining the patterns of belief that the systems were built to serve and which they perpetuate. By taking a conscious look at the beliefs and assumptions we take for granted, we allow ourselves to decide whether we truly agree

---

[4] Schwartz, "Practical Wisdom," *supra*, p.61.

with them. We give ourselves the opportunity to accept the given or make a new choice.

The importance of the frame the parties choose for their relationship and decision making is greater than one might expect. The context set by the frame has a strong influence on how each party sees themselves in relation to one another and the wider world. Providing an intentional context for how to judge options and decisions has profound impact on behavior. In one recent study, merely changing the name of a game from "Wall Street Game" to "Community Game" measurably and significantly impacted whether the participants made self-serving or cooperative choices in the classic "prisoner's dilemma" game. In this study, researchers set for participants a prisoner's dilemma situation in which cooperation would make everyone better off, but by choosing to cooperate the individual would become vulnerable to a "turncoat" (someone who chose not to cooperate). In explaining the game, researchers told participants the title of the game they would be playing. Participants who were told they'd be playing the "Wall Street Game" were measurably more likely to turncoat, while those playing the "Community Game" were more likely to choose cooperation. Same game, same exact rules, but different behavior based on how the activity was characterized solely by its title. Similarly, participants told they were helping with a "Business Transaction Study" were more likely to try and get as much money as they could in contrast to those in the "Social Exchange Study" who focused on "doing what was right."[5]

Choosing the frame means setting the picture off from its surroundings within the greater context of the business world and marketplace. Frame informs choices and impacts behavioral responses. It influences priorities and even more importantly, impacts how parties characterize their relationship. Are they

[5] Liberman, V. "The Name of the Game: Predictive Power of Reputations versus Situational Labels in Determining Prisoner's Dilemma Game Moves." *Personality and Social Psychology Bulletin* 30.9 (2004): 1175–1185.

opponents? Or a community? A cultural set of norms apply to "doing business," and this largely subconscious, default frame triggers noncooperative, me-first logic and behavior. It is expected that a business person is hard-nosed, holding others at arms-length, clinically unemotional and rational, placing financial evaluation above all other values. By consciously exploring which norms the parties would prefer to work with, we can help them intentionally choose and commit to the principles and values that will form an intentional and consciously chosen context for all their decisions and actions.

CHAPTER 4

Introducing Discovering Agreement—Frame and Framework

The legal system embodies the framework, the *structure* within which we engage agreement and dispute. The framework arises from the frame, the context of cultural beliefs. Culture is emblematic of a community's values and comprises their attitudes, beliefs, behaviors, customs, and institutions. Our legal system and the practices associated with it are a reflection of how our culture sees agreement and dispute.

Discovering Agreement (DA) is an alternative approach to formal legal relationships that encourages parties to make conscious choices about frame and framework. Rather than merely looking *through* the frame—the default cultural frame that sets a perspective for adversarial relations—DA practitioners and clients begin by looking *at* the frame. Parties to a contract become coauthors of their own intentional culture, making deliberate choices about which values, beliefs, and structures will shape the context for planning, decision making, and evaluating what is important and what will be their key focal points.

It is important to become conscious of the frame we are using to edit and interpret our understanding of our situation and relationship, because the frame endows meaning; it draws us to conclusions that inform our choices for interaction. By examining the frame, we illuminate premises and unconscious assumptions about proportion, about relationship, and about depth and scope.

DA reframes both the formation conversation and the ongoing conversation between the parties as they perform the contract, in terms of perspectives and guiding principles. The DA contract document—the parties' "Statement of Agreement"[1]—provides a framework that supports the parties' intentional shift in perspective from adversarial to cocreative, continuously reorienting them away from former, habitual patterns and mindsets by providing them with a structure for codesigning and maintaining their ideal working relationship. Thus, DA perspective and principles facilitate the parties as they establish a unique, proprietary frame and framework for how they will assess options, make decisions, engage disagreement between themselves, and make the course corrections needed to achieve and sustain the beneficial purpose of their contractual relationship.

Developing this framework can involve a different kind of attention than most parties are accustomed to giving contract negotiations. It also may take a bit more time at the outset of the relationship. However, most parties find that the initial effort is amply offset by the increased agility, adaptability, and resiliency created for their relationship through establishing a robust platform of trust and alignment.

Overview of the Elements: Touchstone, "ACED," and Condition Precedent

Traditionally, we approach contract negotiation and drafting with

---

[1] I try to avoid calling the contract document "the Agreement." The agreement is something that exists between the parties and the contract document is the memorialization in writing of their agreement. As a way to reinforce awareness of the distinction between the document and the relationship, I use "Statement of Agreement" in place of "the Agreement" to designate the contract document (where possible).

the belief that if we get the deal points properly clarified and written, then the contractual language will prevent unexpected and unwanted behaviors and keep everyone on track. Failing that, we figure the contract will be useful to bring wanderers back on track by defining what's "right" and what's "wrong" behavior, and—if need be—by petitioning a court to force compliance.

With the conventional approach, it is generally assumed that the deal points define the parties' relationship. DA, however, recognizes an important distinction. While the deal points form the parties' action plan for reaching their agreed goals, the deal points are not *the relationship*. The relationship is how the parties relate to one another, how they interact, whether and to what extent they understand and honor one another's needs and intentions. Negotiation is the opportunity to design the plan for achieving the goal(s), to establish an intentional frame and framework for how the parties want to interact and relate to one another in good times and bad, and to explore and clarify the core intentions and imperatives that will inform all of their decisions going forward.

In conventional negotiations, the parties and their attorneys focus on the conversation about deal points and let the back and forth of the negotiation experience become the formative basis of the parties' relationship. By contrast, the DA contract formation conversation begins from a different point than haggling over deal points, looking instead at exploring the parties' core vision and values and calibrating the alignment (or nonalignment) of their joint and respective missions and key interests. While clarifying milestones, deliverables, rights, and duties is important to a smooth transaction or venture, DA seizes the opportunity at the outset of the relationship to investigate and confirm whether the parties are in alignment at the most fundamental and profound level. They are discovering whether they agree about what should be the guiding principles by which decisions are made, proposals are assessed, next steps agreed, and results measured.

Step 1: The Touchstone (the Frame)

The first step in DA is to explore and express in writing the key elements of the perspective and context within which each party operates. I call this written expression "the Touchstone."[2] Usually, it appears as a statement at the beginning of the contract document, similar to the more typical "Recitations," except that it comprises the parties' respective and mutual "Vision, Mission, and Values" statement for their bargain and relationship.

Before proceeding, I want to be clear. The words vision, mission, and values are common in the field of organizational leadership; so much so, that it is important to elucidate what they mean when used in the context of DA conversations and contracts. An in-depth exploration is reserved for later, but for now suffice it to say that the Touchstone is not a repeat or rehash of the corporate mission statements commonly found on home pages and annual report covers (and apparently devised mostly for public-relations effect). It is, by contrast, a carefully constructed declaration of the basic truths and core principles that the parties have intentionally identified as their guide and focal point for times when they come together to deal with disruptive change, rising tensions, and full-blown disagreement.

The key purpose of the Touchstone comprising the statement of the parties' Vision, Mission, and Values is to bring transparency and clarity about what really matters to them. The investigation and expression of their Touchstone provision becomes the foundation for mutual comprehension and a shared frame of meaning which the parties can use when assessing proposals, options, and decisions. It forms the "design

---

[2] A touchstone, literally, is a piece of basalt or jasper used to test the purity of gold or silver. Its more common meaning these days is, a standard or criterion by which something is judged or recognized.

specifications" for how their relationship and coendeavor will be conducted— identifying and expressly stating how they will focus their lens when looking at any issue. The written Touchstone becomes a key tool as their relationship proceeds, reminding them of what really matters and to focus, or refocus, accordingly.

Clients and attorneys may be concerned about the "extra time" needed to develop a meaningful Touchstone, but taking time to consciously examine the frame through which each party sees the world is worthwhile. The frame through which we view the world directly and powerfully affects our circumstances because it dictates how we interpret the words and deeds of others. In turn, our interpretation of the meaning behind another's actions informs our reasoning about logical and appropriate responses and reactions.

In his book, *The Speed of Trust*, Steven M. R. Covey, points out that we tend to judge others by their behavior and ourselves by our intentions.[3] When change brings disruption or crisis, we tend to seek a response that can be called fair. The aspiration for fairness is universal. Achieving fairness is a huge challenge largely because of what Joshua Greene identifies in his book, *Moral Tribes*, as "the fairness bias" that is built into each perspective.[4] Research shows that when study participants know which side of a dispute they are on, their definition of what is a fair outcome shifts to favor that side's needs and perspective.[5] Knowing which side one is on changes the way one processes information.[6] Fairness is illusive and ephemeral.

This seems like an insurmountable problem, until we consider

---

[3] Covey, Stephen M. R., and Rebecca R. Merrill. *The Speed of Trust: The One Thing That Changes Everything.* New York: Free Press, 2008. Print.

[4] Greene, Joshua David. *Moral Tribes: Emotion, Reason, and the Gap between Us and Them.* 1st ed. Penguin, 2013. pp.83–89. Print.

[5] Ibid.

[6] Ibid. "[I]t seems that knowing which side of a dispute you're on unconsciously changes your thinking about what's fair. It changes the way you process information." p.85.

the possibility of doing away with "sides" to the dispute. Rather than try to set up a system that will reliably deliver "fair" outcomes (impossible), we can set up a system for coevaluation of whether a proposed action or outcome is aligned with what really matters to the parties—starting with a conscious effort made at the outset to clarify and confirm the frame each party is using to interpret meaning within their relationship. Without this clarity and confirmation, then even in the early stage of negotiation, the parties' relationship is at increased risk of breaking down due to misinterpretation of actions and misperception of motives and intentions.

Even if it only goes so far as one lawyer and her/his client getting clear about that client's core Vision, Mission, and Values, having this Touchstone conversation is worthwhile. Knowing what really matters and having a clearly articulated, written[7] Touchstone that continually reminds and realigns the client with their foundational intentions gives both attorney and client a valuable tool for assessing proposals and options and resisting the temptation to respond in kind to emotional provocation. Both lawyer and client are less susceptible to the trap of seeking fairness; they need only check for alignment with what really matters to the client.

For the parties, getting clear with each other about alignment of Vision, Mission, and Values can save a great deal of time and effort in the long run. To begin with, they learn early on if the working relationship is not a good fit—saving time and energy at the outset. In addition, when each understands their own and the

---

[7] Clarity about the Touchstone and putting it in writing are valuable even if the Touchstone and conversational structure provisions are not incorporated into the ultimate contract document. It is my experience that lawyers and their clients gain a great deal by consciously exploring and determining what really matters to each party with respect to short and long-term goals, the unique value and purpose of joining forces with the other party (as opposed to joining forces with someone else or going it alone), the keys to a satisfactory working relationship, and—even more deeply—the core values and visions that motivate each of them and inform all of their decisions.

other's deeper motivations, the parties have a broader scope for finding solutions to crisis and conflict between themselves. They have a greater chance of creating and sustaining value in the bargain and relationship, a better chance of creating an action plan that will work for everyone in both the short- and long-terms, and each has less chance of misunderstanding the reasons why the other party takes actions or makes choices in the course of the relationship (the kinds of misunderstandings that lead to unnecessary conflict).

All of this lowers the likelihood that disputes will arise during the course of the relationship, and if disagreement does occur, the parties have a shorter road to recovering understanding and agreement and restoring the trust crucial to successful and enjoyable relationships, because they have built their deal and plan on a foundation of true and meaningful understanding of everyone's needs, expectations, and motivations.

Reframing the conversation generates a new kind of conversation very different from the competitive, adversarial negotiation focused solely on winning advantage and shifting burdens through persuasion, manipulation, or coercion. It is a conversation to discover whether they are sufficiently aligned in purpose and values to establish and sustain a successful, enjoyable, and worthwhile working relationship.

The Function of a Contract

A typical contract serves two essential functions.

1. *Clarifying Expectations.* The parties clarify and express their expectations and systems for conducting the transactional relationship—who will do what, by when, in what manner, and how will the results and proceeds of their efforts (risks, losses, gains) be allocated; and

2. *Dealing with Disruption.* The contract should simplify and streamline how the parties manage disruptive change and disagreement—how issues are identified, how

parties are notified, and how the conflict is engaged and resolved.

Notice that the first function addresses who, what, when, where, and how. All are very necessary elements to any contract. The Touchstone adds a third essential function: *why*. And this is crucial. The Touchstone can illuminate *why* one party and not the other has certain responsibilities, *why* the time frame is important, *why* the manner in which the job is done matters, and *why* the allocation of the results makes sense. This sets the stage for success when disruption occurs. Because both parties clearly understand why the original specifications were put in place, they are in a much better position to make adjustments when things do not go as planned.

The power of knowing "why" crystallized for me when I heard Dominic Barter tell the story of an agreement reached between a bakery cashier and the young man who had held up the bakery. The agreement was the culmination of a Restorative Circle[8] process that brought the young man and the cashier together to address the impact of the robbery on everyone involved, the conditions that gave rise to the robbery, and to enable circle participants to create a plan for moving forward in restored community and harmony. Part of the resulting Action Plan involved the cashier's request that the young man return to the bakery three times as a customer. The cashier explained that his sense of safety in his workplace had been shattered by the robbery, and the young man's return as a customer would help the cashier recover his sense of safety.

The reality of the situation was that the young man who had committed the robbery was taken from the circle conversation to jail where he served his required time—about a year. When he was released, Dom told me, the young man went to the bakery to

---

[8] Barter, Dominic. "An Introduction to Restorative Circles with Dominic Barter." *Vimeo*. https:// vimeo.com/user2006436, 2010. Web. 23 Aug. 2015.; www.restorativecircles.org

fulfill that part of the Action Plan only to learn that the cashier no longer worked in that place. He could have satisfied the technical requirements of the Action Plan by patronizing the bakery three times, but this young man—as a result of the circle conversation—knew and understood the meaning of the cashier's request. So he found out where the cashier's new workplace was, and he visited that place three times as a customer. Knowing and connecting with the why behind the "visit three times" provision in their agreement meant that the young man did not merely fulfill the minimum technical requirements to discharge his obligation; it meant that he looked beyond the "four corners" of the agreement terms and served the purpose for which their Action Plan was designed.

Expressing the Touchstone clearly enhances the contract's first function by exploring and clarifying the meaning behind the parties' choices and actions; but what about the second function—dealing with disruption? All this mutual understanding can be reassuring, even energizing, but how do the parties know they can trust it? How can they feel confident that everyone is being upfront about their true motivations and goals, and how can anyone be confident they trust the other party will walk their talk when the chips are down? The parties need some way to build into the contract a meaningful commitment on the part of all participants to honor and abide by their foundational Vision, Mission, and Values.

Step 2: Addressing Change and Engaging Disagreement

The second step in DA is putting in place a framework for those courageous, cocreative conversations when the parties need to address a disruptive change or crisis or when they have an actual disagreement. This framework for conversation is linked to the Touchstone in that the parties agree their conflict conversation will focus on how they can bring themselves back into alignment with the Touchstone. And the framework provides a roadmap for how they will navigate and solve the problem they face according to what really matters to them both. In this way the parties establish a "peace-provoking"[9] system that will exert pressure to encourage them and support them in collaborative, productive responses rather than driving them toward escalating adversarial and destructive reactions.

In my experience, this supporting framework has three essential components:

i. a commitment to engage in structured dialogue,
ii. an agreement that all decisions, plans, and resolutions will be assessed based on how well they align with the Touchstone, and
iii. a crucial "condition precedent."

The reality is that every relationship experiences conflict. From time to time, the parties will very likely need to have conversations about disappointed expectations, about disagreements, or about changed circumstances that drive one or the other to rethink the plan—conversations likely to be fraught with emotion. With DA, they agree ahead of time, in writing, about how they will organize and hold these conversations. Rather than imagine we can prevent or preresolve every conflict by setting up rules, incentives, and penalties, DA takes the perspective that it is better to prepare for safe and productive conflict by setting in place the criteria for evaluating situations and making wise judgment calls collaboratively.

The first crucial step is to realize that *conflict need not be adversarial.* Conflict is as natural as thunder and rain. The fact that two parties are experiencing conflict does not mean they are necessarily opponents. Conflict is feedback telling the parties that they are participants in a Commons—a community—and

---

[9] Crosby, Michelle. "Peace Provoking An Oxymoron?" *Life::Wevorce.* Wevorce, 3 Aug. 2013. Web. 27 Aug. 2015.

something important has happened, something needs updating. To borrow from the world of software development, they've found a bug in their program and need to codesign a fix that works for everyone. Reframing conflict changes how it impacts behaviors and helps set a new, productive logic pattern in place.

However, having the intention to adopt a new mindset about what conflict means and actually meeting conflict in a new way can be two very different things. Most of us need support to reorient our approach when we are in the midst of the actual experience of conflict. DA parties intentionally and specifically designate a structured process to do this *before* the conflict ever arises.

The DA contract serves to support the fundamental shift away from adversarial mindsets by setting out a basic structure— chosen by the parties—for how rising tensions will be brought to the parties' mutual attention and how they will conduct their conflicts. This framework provides a roadmap uniquely suited to the needs of the parties, one that they can use to guide themselves (or navigate with the help of a designated facilitator) through a process of cocreative problem solving and conflict resolution. In short, the DA Statement of Agreement sets out the parties' own system for responding to disruptive change, giving them tools to deal with whatever comes along rather than trying to forecast and control an unpredictable future. I have come to call this section of the contract, the Addressing Change and Engaging Disagreement provision (ACED).

Inside the ACED

The first component of the ACED provision is a mutual commitment by the parties that should they find themselves in disagreement, they will engage in dialogue directed towards finding a way to stay in, or return to, alignment with the Touchstone.

"Dialogue" is another word that embodies multiple meanings.

In the context of DA, the promise to engage in dialogue is a commitment by the parties to engage in the ACED conversation as equals, with no "my way or the highway," preconceived outcome, listening with a willingness to be influenced and changed by what they hear.

Alone, this commitment to engage in dialogue is not enough. When tensions rise and trust is diminished (as is generally the case when parties are in conflict with one another), the willingness and ability to engage in meaningful dialogue can be seriously compromised. To go beyond an aspirational declaration and actually be practicable in the heat of the moment, the commitment needs structural support. For this reason, ACED provisions should also include expressly designated and specific steps that the parties agree to follow whenever one or both need to call an ACED dialogue about rising tensions, emerging problems, disruptive change, or full-blown conflict between themselves. In my experience, if specific steps are missing, the DA framework is unstable and can quickly collapse.

In addition to step-by-step instructions for calling and conducting the conflict conversation, the parties further agree in the ACED provisions that their dialogue will focus on bringing about whatever transformation is required for the deal/plan/relationship to remain or return to alignment with their declared Touchstone statement. In this way, the Touchstone becomes the agreed framing perspective that the parties will use to evaluate problems, actions, options, and decisions.

In sum, using the contractual ACED provisions, the parties set in place a system designed to their specifications to ensure they can capably engage conflict amongst themselves (either on their own or with the help of a designated facilitator) in a way that makes serving the declared Touchstone imperative. They commit to engaging conflict by participating in structured dialogue dedicated to solving for alignment with the Touchstone rather than by solving for whose preferred solution will be imposed upon the other.

Accountability

Another important function of contracts is to ensure that the parties are accountable for their actions. The concept of accountability tends to carry a connotation of "enforcement" (which requires an authoritative enforcer). We hold someone accountable by making them pay to even a score. This has the flavor of a coercive mindset antithetical to the autonomy and self-determination that are core values in DA, so it is important to clarify the meaning of "accountability" in the DA context.

DA accountability derives from the parties' voluntary commitment to align their respective and joint actions with the guiding principles that comprise the Touchstone. When crisis erupts, our habitual mindset and the conventional system pit the parties as adversaries. Lawyers and parties look to the contract, mining it for weapons they can use to force the other side to take or refrain from certain actions. An inevitable by-product of this conventional structure is that in the battle over conflicting interpretations of terms and provisions, the reason the parties decided to work together is subverted, and their beneficial relationship destroyed. By contrast, the ACED provisions are designed to evoke meaningful dialogue.

The ACED provision addresses the need for accountability by integrating the Touchstone statement into the designated dispute resolution system that the parties construct for themselves and describe in the contract. The designated conversational structure supports accountability by establishing the Touchstone as the measure of suitability for any decisions/plans proposed in the course of their dialogue. The parties have committed and agreed to be accountable to what really matters to them. This creates a new spaciousness and agility in moments of crisis. They no longer need to battle within the confines of language written in the past and inadequate to new realities but can, together, update or redesign their endeavor to better serve the purposes its original plan no longer suits, without losing their commitment to what matters most.

At this point in the DA process—as they create their system for organizing and conducting conflict—the parties are actually able to test whether they really have discovered common ground. A party who has not been totally forthcoming or completely sincere about their Vision, Mission, and Values statements will, at this juncture, realize that there is no upside to equivocation in the Touchstone statement. Their Touchstone is the ultimate arbiter of "good and bad," "right and wrong," "okay and not okay," and if they have not been accurate or complete in their contribution to the Touchstone, they are only cheating themselves of the opportunity to found all decisions on what really matters to them.

The DA contract embodies the parties' own proprietary system, which also must interface effectively with the larger conventional system. It is not enough for the parties to contractually declare their capacity for self-determination. Their private law must work well within the larger, existing system. The third component of the DA contractual structure helps the parties leverage the conventions of contract law to establish and sustain their customized, proprietary system for self-governance and decision making.

Step 3: Condition Precedent

To secure their commitment to walking their talk, DA parties accept a contractual commitment to engage in their designated form of Touchstone-centric, problem-solving dialogue as a precondition to pursuing any other form of dispute resolution, including litigation. It is generally understood that parties cannot contract away their right to litigate. This does not, however, preclude creating an enforceable obligation to at least try the

ACED dialogue first.[10] In the DA Statement of Agreement document, the effort to restore alignment with one another in accordance with the Touchstone is an express "condition precedent" to initiating adversarial proceedings.

This condition precedent feature is, admittedly, paradoxical. If one party starts out of the gate by ignoring the Touchstone and the agreed structure for cocreative conversation, but instead goes directly to an adversarial approach (filing suit), the other party will be able to show the court that there is a binding, contractual obligation for the parties to first engage the defined and described restorative, nonadversarial process. In this way, ironically, the conventional, coercive system is used to compel the parties to at least attempt to walk the talk of their Touchstone and try a nonadversarial, restorative, creative, problem-solving approach before they resort to destructive adversarial proceedings.

It may be, in the end, one party is so dedicated to an adversarial approach that the ACED conversation becomes a mere formality, but what is there to lose by trying? If the ACED dialogue is attempted, there is a much greater chance that the parties will reach a mutually satisfactory, amicable resolution without destructive, expensive litigation. They might even end up with a stronger relationship based on a cocreated, realigned, new and improved action plan. This sort of outcome is not

---

[10] Case law has established that parties who agree to arbitration have (in most instances) relinquished their right to litigation in the courts. *Oxford Health Plans LLC v. Sutter,* 133 S.Ct. 2064 (2013); *StoltNielsen S.A. v. AnimalFeeds Int'l Corp.,* 559 U.S. 662, 130 S.Ct. 1758, 1775 (enforceability of arbitration clause requires mutual consent of the parties to resolve disputes by arbitration); *see generally,* Silvergreenberg, Jessica, and Robert Gebeloff. "Arbitration Everywhere, Stacking the Deck of Justice." *The New York Times.* The New York Times, 31 Oct. 2015; and Gillies, Peter S., and Andrew Dahdal. "Waiver of a Right to Arbitrate by Resort to Litigation, in the Context of International Commercial Arbitration." *Journal of International Commercial Law and Technology* 2.4 (2007): 221–30 (discussion of enforceability of arbitration clauses in context of international commercial arbitration).

usually a viable possibility when the primary go-to system for addressing conflict is adversarial proceedings.

It is also true that a party may choose to just walk away, to terminate the relationship without engaging the ACED conversation. Again, if this is the case, the DA parties are no worse off than they would have been with conventional dispute resolution provisions. If someone is hell-bent on adversarial proceedings, the hell of litigation will always be available.

In sum:

1. DA begins during the initial negotiations—using a practice of conscious exploration and calibration of the parties' overall visions, their core values and guiding principles, and the mission they are joining forces to accomplish—resulting in a written expression that serves as a Touchstone for decision making and problem solving.

2. The next step is to memorialize their understanding in words, drafting it as part of their contract—and also codifying in writing their commitment to staying in alignment with the stated Touchstone—designating a conversational structure for dealing with disputes that arise between the parties.

3. The third step is the parties' express agreement that before they resort to adversarial methods of any kind, they will engage in their designated collaborative process, and their conversations will focus on coming back into alignment with the stated Vision, Mission, and Values Touchstone.

With DA, the parties' relationship is based on aligned and expressed goals, visions, and expectations. The deal points comprise their plan for accomplishing with integrity the mission that the relationship is created to carry out. Because parties involved in a DA conversation have explored what really matters to each of them, they have an understanding of what is meaningful, worthwhile, and crucial to one another. By taking time to clarify the why that underlies the contract terms, they have established a relationship of mutual comprehension and understanding. This genuine relationship means that they have a better ability to execute their plan and, if need be, adjust it. If they have included DA provisions in their formal contract document, then they will be able to use their proprietary system for engaging disagreement and making course corrections as needed to continue pursuit of their shared and respective overarching goals. The plan doesn't govern them; they govern the plan—together.

SECTION II

This section turns from the broader, conceptual dimensions of Discovering Agreement (DA) to the practical realm of what it is like to actually engage clients, other parties (and their counsel) in a DA conversation.

The practice of DA is a path of learning, not of knowing. What follows is based on my own experiences and experiences of others who practice their own versions of "values based contracts." As John O'Donohue said, "The great questions never settle to sleep inside answers."[1] The work of DA is to choose and to remain faithful to the questions that light the path.

---

[1] O'Donohue, John. "Toward a Poetics of Possibility." *An Easter People: Essays in Honor of Sr. Stanislaus Kennedy.* Ed. Stanislaus Kennedy and John Scally. Dublin, Ireland: Veritas, 2005. Print.

CHAPTER 5

Touchstone

From the DA perspective, the deal points do not define the parties' relationship. Deal points comprise the Action Plan that the parties create for pursuing their joint and several purposes. The relationship is how they relate to one another as they implement their Action Plan—how they treat one another, work together, and how they interact with each other and with the wider world. In conventional practice, we tend to just start relating and see what develops. DA begins with consciously considering what the parties' ideal working relationship would be and intentionally designing it to their particular specifications for success and sustainability.

Businesses need trustworthy relationships. There is an efficiency that comes with trust. Kit Miller, Director of the Gandhi Institute for Nonviolence, reminds us of how quickly decisions can be made and actions taken when we are working with people we trust and, by contrast, how labored and painful it is to try and make progress on even the most inconsequential decisions when the parties don't trust one another.[1]

When parties enjoy a trusting and trustworthy relationship, they become a strong and agile cooperative unit. Effective cooperation confers a competitive edge, allowing the parties to join forces (knowledge, experience, resources, etc.) and increase their capacities to survive and flourish in the ever-changing,

---

[1] "The Efficiency of Trust: Capacity Building for Effective Change." *YouTube.* MEL Talks at Meliora Weekend 2014, 13 Mar. 2015. Web. 28 Aug. 2015. Featuring Kit Miller, Director of the M.K. Gandhi Institute for Nonviolence.

ever-challenging marketplace. Trust is based on credibility, and credibility relies on integrity—knowing that you can rely on the person you are dealing with to be honest about intent and values and to follow through on those by always aligning their actions with their declared intentions and values.[2]

It is important at the outset for each party to confirm that this is a relationship they *want* to enter and one that they feel confident is trustworthy. Neither party necessarily needs the other to adopt, in full, their particular values, vision, or mission. However, they do need to know what is at the root of one another's choices. We can expect people to act in accordance with what truly matters to them. They may turn to contract terms to rationalize or justify what they want to do or what has been done, but action is not motivated by the existence of the contract terms as much as it is driven by the compelling realities of their (conscious or unconscious) needs and interests. Gaining conscious awareness of the underlying motivations that are most likely to impact decisions and actions will help the parties better understand the meaning and purpose of proposals and choices that they present to one another. It also helps the parties know whether they are sufficiently aligned to establish a sustainable and sturdy foundation for working together productively—will they be pulling in the same direction on the things that really matter?

In addition to calibrating their mutual alignment, gaining clarity about key values and interests will help the parties as they conduct their relationship in the fishbowl environment of global, digital connectivity. The transparent digital marketplace demands that companies "walk their talk." In other words, the transparency and immediacy of global, digital communications requires that companies act with integrity—"integrity" being *consciously aligning actions with deeply held values.* If a company has not declared a set of values, then the global community will supply cultural values that the company

---

[2] Covey, *The Speed of Trust, supra.*

"should" align with. If they have declared vision, mission, and values, then any action that appears to be in conflict with those exposes the company to ready and, on occasion, virulent criticism. To act with integrity, one has to know what one's key/core values are and have systemic support for staying in alignment with them—a way for everyone in the company and the contractual relationship to orient actions (words and deeds) with integrity—because the Internet is watching.

What Really Matters

It seems simplistic, but when parties really think about it, they generally realize they are surprisingly unclear about what really matters to them. We think we know what is driving our decision making, but when we sit down and try to express it in writing, we discover that we haven't been totally conscious about what are truly our core ideals and interests. In the business setting, people tend to assume that what really matters to the company are the default values culture assigns to business—return on investment for shareholders, growth and profit. In the emerging world of socially responsible, "conscious" business, however, many companies and the people they comprise have additional, compelling visions, purposes, and values.[3] The Touchstone is the opportunity for the parties to put in writing an expression of their respective and their shared core interests and ideals. Their Touchstone clarifies and confirms the criteria that the parties actually (really) use when assessing their options, their actions, and their decisions, and when solving their problems.

When I work with clients, I generally break the Touchstone

---

[3] "Triple Bottom Line." *The Economist*. The Economist Newspaper, 17 Nov. 2009. Web. 27 Aug. 2015. (online article adapted from "The Economist Guide to Management Ideas and Gurus", Hindle, Tim. London: Profile, 2008. Print.); "TriplePundit: Reporting on the Triple Bottom Line & Sustainable Business News." *Triple Pundit People Planet Profit*. Triple Pundit, LLC., Web. 27 Aug. 2015.

down into four basic elements:

1. Vision: The Big Why
2. Mission: The Purpose of the Contractual Relationship (particular mission + reasons for choosing this particular partner)
3. Values & Principles: Keys to Satisfaction
4. Constraints & Imperatives: Boundaries

These terms "Vision, Mission, and Values" get used a lot in business, and they mean a lot of different things to a lot of different people. Hence, the lawyer in me says, let's be clear about definition of terms.

Vision: The Big Why

Some people (lawyers and clients alike) find it difficult to believe there is real value in exploring a seemingly esoteric question such as a person's (or company's) most profound aspirations for their contribution to the world, but I have found it is important to try and understand why we do what we do. Lack of awareness diminishes our ability to make intentional choices. When something is unconscious, it is still acting on the person, and it is at that point they are not in full choice. Something unexpected happens, and suddenly they are making decisions intuitively without conscious awareness of what's at the root of that "intuitive" sensation. There is greater stability and access to wisdom when one is aware of the core drivers for one's decisions and desires. Conscious awareness of, and connection to, one's deep motivation becomes a source of strength upon which one can call when things get confusing, difficult, or just plain dull.

Vision tells us what the party stands for, what is the better world they can envision, their "cause." I shy away from words like "purpose" and "aspiration" when talking about a client's vision because it is easy to get too small an answer using those words. "What is the purpose of your business?" often triggers the nearly automatic response "To make money." And "What is your aspiration?" tends to lead to answers like, "To become the industry leader." These responses are about results and goals. Vision, to be useful in the Touchstone, should speak to something far bigger and deeper than return on investment and competitive dominance.

Vision is about *meaning*. When we ask about vision we are wondering, what is the point? Why am I here? Why do this work? We all ask these types of questions. We ask them because we have an innate need to connect with the underlying meaning in our experiences. Viktor Frankl's book, *Man's Search for Meaning*, is a perennial bestseller because, as he himself said, "[I]f hundreds of thousands of people reach out for a book whose very title promises to deal with the question of a meaning to life, it must be a question that burns under their very fingernails."[4]

Without a connection to meaning, things don't make sense, so we seek for something that will help us make sense—something that will give us a handle on what is happening (or what happened in the past). In our work and our relationships, if something happens and we are not already connected with a meaning, we will choose a meaning and attach it to the experience. The meaning we choose will affect how we interact with others in the relationship or those who in some way share in the experience.

Realizing that we have a say in the meaning of our experience gives us great power. By exploring the question of meaning, we uncover many areas of our lives in which we have unwittingly adopted a questionable template. When we start to observe our reflexive responses, we discover where we have abdicated our power, given it over to cultural norms, societal structures and systems, or other inherited traditions. We become shapers rather

---

[4] Frankl, Viktor E. *Man's Search for Meaning*. New York: Washington Square/Pocket, 1985. Print. p.15.

than victims of circumstances.

Taking back our power requires us to become alert and notice when our autopilot kicks in. We must look for and question the assumptions that inform the meaning we assign to the actions of others, to our own choices, to the work we do, and to our relationships. Rather than blindly adopting conventional templates, we can examine them and discover whether we agree with the assigned meaning or if there is another way of understanding the situation—a way that better serves us. This is how we leave the realm of victims and perpetrators and enter into a powerful engagement with life as creators.

Our cultural norms and social structures often assign a template for us, prescribing a meaning to our experiences and defining us as powerful or powerless. Much of the time we don't even notice whether the assigned template is accurate, useful, or healthy for us. We are conditioned to frame our experiences in accordance with our culture's conventional mindset. By consciously exploring the Vision, Mission, and Values, as well as the constraints and imperatives that we are using as our template for making sense of our experiences and circumstances, we give ourselves the opportunity to blaze the path we want rather than following one laid out by and for others.

It can be remarkably difficult to articulate this sort of vision. Few people are able to create a meaningful vision statement without some assistance. There are several techniques for investigating the question. In "Moral Tribes," Joshua Greene suggests that one "start with the things that you care about most immediately and then work backward, repeatedly asking yourself, 'why do I care about that?' until you run out of answers."[5] Dr. M. Scott Peck invented what he called the "so-that game" in which you say, "I want [x] so that..." and keep on answering "so-that" until you reach the ultimate reason.[6] And

---

[5] Greene, Moral Tribes, *supra,* p.160.
[6] Peck, M. Scott. In Search of Stones: *A Pilgrimage of Faith, Reason, and Discovery.* New York: Hyperion, 1995. Print.

Stephen M. R. Covey recommends the "five whys" technique—asking "why" five times in a row as a way to discover real intent.[7]

These are all versions of a technique that works along these lines:

1. Why do you want to require only organic ingredients be used in the products?

   To encourage the global adoption of organic agricultural practices.

2. Why is that something you want to encourage?

   Organic agriculture produces food in a way that establishes and maintains ecological balance.

3. Why is that important?

   It means providing food while also reducing (and hopefully eliminating) the use of synthetic chemical pesticides.

4. Why do you believe synthetic chemicals and other nonorganic agricultural practices need to be eliminated?

   We believe that the use of synthetic chemicals and other nonorganic agricultural practices is linked to increased pollution and illness, while organic practices restore and sustain the environment.

5. And that is important to you because…?

   Because we believe the world's food can be grown in plenty without causing harm to the planet. We believe we all share a responsibility to restore and sustain a healthy global environment and habitat for all living beings.

Another way to start the exploration is by asking the "miracle" question: If you woke up tomorrow and a miracle had happened and the key problem that you see with our world had been fixed, what would be different, what would people be

---

[7] *The Speed of Trust, supra* p. 86.

doing?

The Vision statement describes that miraculously better world that the person (or group) can see, that they can imagine. The better world they can envision is the thing that is behind their ranting when they get really angry about the state of the world and behind their despair when they get really sad. Behind every rant about some idiocy or injustice is a vision of a better world. It is that vision of a better way things could be that we are trying to put into words as a Vision statement.

When drafting a Vision statement, be sure to ask yourself whether the person or group has described an "incentive" (certain monetary milestone/ threshold) or a "position," as opposed to a transcendent vision. Vision is something beyond positions, strategies, games, milestones, and status.

It is easy to mistake a "position" for a "vision." Be aware of the distinction between taking a position and understanding the underlying interests. To do this, I keep asking, "Why?"

Here are some examples of Position versus Vision:

Position: The artists must control the final decisions about which of their artworks appear on the gallery's website and how the works are presented within the site.

Why? What interests do you believe would be served if you had sole control of these decisions? You want to control these decisions so that...

Vision: We envision a showplace where each artist's unique vision is honored and valued and where the audience can trust that the experience they encounter is the authentic experience that the artist intended to offer.

* * *

Position: Every ingredient we use in the candy we sell must be organically and locally grown.

Why? What is the reason this is so important?

Vision: We envision a world where food is cultivated, harvested, and marketed in a way that sustains the health and beauty of the planet and all living beings. It is a world where our efforts in support of this provide each of us a livelihood that is meaningful, fun, and financially viable.[8]

When their vision for a better world is clear, the parties can create goals that are aligned with their respective and shared visions and become a part of creating the world in which they want to live. Knowing the vision enables them to be less susceptible to getting involved in missions or projects that cultural or systemic pressures indicate they "should" be doing. With a firm grasp on the world they want to be a part of creating, they have a broader understanding of how to define "success," and can begin to craft their missions and choose the people and companies as partners that are going to meaningfully and reliably contribute to that success.

Example Vision Statement

Vision – We envision a world where all manufacturing processes are environmentally healthy and sustainable without sacrificing the quality of the ensuing products, the health and well-being of the people who make them, or the health and well-being of purchasers and the wider community.

Mission: The Purpose of the Contractual Relationship

Mission is where we clarify the particular project, business, or transaction that the parties are entering together and the key goals they intend to achieve by joining forces.

With the miraculous new world in mind, what are the parties

---

[8] In this example, the first part of the vision statement addresses the values behind the position about ingredients. The second part of the statement acknowledges there is a broader vision that encompasses the well-being of the parties themselves. Articulating this will help the parties create systems that support their enjoyment of the endeavor in addition to the overall vision of a better world.

interested in doing? What *specifically* are they planning to join forces to do to make that miracle happen?

Vision is seeing the world that could be. Mission is focused on the strategic, planned actions the parties intend to take in their efforts to serve their Vision. Mission is how the parties plan to actively participate in moving the world toward the visionary ideal—what they want to put their effort and energy into that will contribute to bringing the envisioned changes.

Let me acknowledge here that many business people have an almost allergic reaction to the phrase "Mission Statement." It comes with so much baggage that I hesitate to use it. The parties may prefer "Intentions" or "Goals" rather than "Mission." What one calls it is less important than the distinction between the content of this statement and that of the "Vision" statement.

It may be helpful to present a sort of "fill in the blank" question to a client:

My mission, in service of this vision, is to *(manufacture widgets?; provide services?; create something? other?)* so that *(name the essential goals you want to achieve – financial? environmental? social? spiritual? other?)*

or

My goals for entering this relationship are _____.

We are joining forces so that _____.

When developing a statement about the relationship's Mission, it may also be helpful to ask the following questions with respect to the miraculous new world that is envisioned:

- What are you [interested in] doing now to make the miracle happen?
- Are pieces of the miracle already happening? If so, what do you [want to] do to keep them going?
- What is this transaction/relationship/endeavor meant to provide in terms of "making the miracle happen" for the world?
- If you can't see how this project or undertaking helps

make the miracle happen, then what is it supposed to make happen?

- Why do you want to enter the relationship? Why do you want to work with this coparty in particular?
- What will change for you, your organization, the world, the community, (etc.) as a result of this transaction/relationship/endeavor?

Beyond defining what a successful mission would look like, it can also be worthwhile to explore the consequences of failure of the mission.

- What if this endeavor doesn't succeed?
- What is "not succeeding"?
- Is it a failure if the mission is not accomplished?
- What about accomplishing the mission in a way that does not serve the vision and/or accord with your values?

Example Mission Statement

(An agreement between Author and Social Media Curator/Website Designer)

Our shared mission is to generate a wider reach and sustained longevity for the Author's message and works, and to support the Author's ongoing work and artistic growth, respecting her wishes regarding work/rest balance and privacy while building a loyal readership and community around her work.

Our shared goals are specifically: steadily increasing sales and website traffic, growth in the burgeoning conversation about the Author's work, care with respect to her wishes to be allowed her peace and privacy, and the creation of a solid foundation for her work's ongoing presence and increasing dissemination.

Values & Principles: Keys to Satisfaction

Know thyself

—Plato

To thine own self be true.
—William Shakespeare (Polonius, Hamlet)

When addressing values and guiding principles, we are essentially talking about the keys to satisfaction. How people should treat one another, and what are the parties' expectations about how they want to be treated and how they expect themselves and the other party to behave. Here is where we are really making a conscious, intentional choice about how the parties will relate to one another.

We cannot easily step outside our individual moral perspectives—if that is even possible—so let's get clear what our respective moral perspectives are and see if they are compatible enough that we can cooperate and honor our own and one another's moral codes. If we can, then we have created a solid platform from which to launch our cooperative efforts. If we can't—don't we want to know that before we commit time and energy and treasure?

Parties can generally provide a laundry list of key values: excellence, responsiveness, professionalism, collegiality, etc. It is useful to examine the list and make sure everyone understands the meaning of words that are open to multiple connotations. For instance, I often hear, "I really value professionalism." But when I ask the parties to explain—to give examples of professionalism or nonprofessionalism—we find out that one party means "keeping emotions out of the conversation" and the other means "showing up on time and being well prepared." This is a good time to talk and really understand—When you say "efficiency," "responsiveness," and "enjoyment" what do you mean?—and to capture those keys to satisfaction in the statement of Values.

A person can only be a jerk or a bully in relation to someone else. The behavior I identify as "bullying" is about my values and expectations around how people behave and how they express unhappiness or disagreement. I'm pretty much guaranteed not to be aware of my own bullying behavior because it doesn't look like bullying from my point of view. I see it as something else, because I know the underlying intentions that are driving my behavior. I can, however, be reminded to compare my values for "playing well with others" against the way I am, in the moment, behaving—and that can help me see that I am not aligning my actions with my own values. Having someone insist that I change my behavior to suit them is remarkably ineffective. I find it much easier to shift my behavior when I realize it does not align with my own values. A statement of Principles & Values helps me recall myself and avoid words and deeds I might later regret.

As with Vision and Mission, when exploring Values it is helpful to use questions, such as,

- How do you like to be treated in the workplace? How do you expect yourself to treat others?
- What are the keys to satisfaction, to your willingness to enter and continue in any working relationship?
- When you think about your favorite working relationships, what was it about them that made them so great?
- When you think about the worst working relationships you've had, what was it that made them so awful?
- How do you expect (require) professionals (yourself and others) to behave in a crisis or when bad news is discovered?
- To what do you wish to habituate yourself?[9]

---

[9] "Habituate" means, "become accustomed to, learn to ignore stimulus, make somebody used to something." Soukhanov, Anne H. Microsoft *Encarta College Dictionary*. New York: St. Martin's, 2001. Print.

In trying to define guiding principles, it can be helpful to ask, "What activities would you consider incompatible with the purpose of this contract and relationship? Getting a statement of incompatible activities will provide information you can use in helping the client craft a positive Values & Principles statement and also for more fully exploring where there are constraints or imperatives that remain unrecognized—our next topic.

Example Values & Principles

Our Values – We value a work setting where each of us has independence, authority, and autonomy to run our individual mission based efforts with our teams while others do the same. We are dedicated to kindness, respect, graciousness and compassion towards ourselves and others in everything we do. We value innovation, courage, adaptability, excellence and having fun. It is important to each of us that we each wake-up excited about the day ahead, interested in the things on our schedules, eager to begin.

Constraints & Imperatives: Boundaries

Are there any things that must never be true, or must always be true for the parties to be willing to enter into and continue in the working relationship? Parties may sincerely intend that their coendeavor, supported by the contractual language, will mean that they work together to do whatever will produce the best overall consequences for everyone— parties plus stakeholders. However, the reality of our sweat-of-the-brow lives is that there will always be tension between what is good for the individual and what is best for all.

"Expectations are resentments waiting to happen."[10] Transparency is a good thing. All parties should be clear about

---

[10] Lamott, Anne. *Crooked Little Heart.* New York: Pantheon, 1997. Print.

their real bottom line. It could be just a financial bottom line, such as, if they are not making a certain return on investment, then they will want out. Making that clear for everyone—lawyer, client, and the other party—can avert serious misalignment of expectations.[11]

Constraints are things that one or more parties will never agree to or abide with. They are boundaries that must not be crossed. Imperatives are things that must always be true or present. They are the guiding principles that must never be violated.

Questions to help reveal unspoken Constraints & Imperatives:

- What are the boundaries that must not be crossed?
- Is there something that is so important to you that having it or preventing it would trump your other obligations?

For instance, some people say that they put family first. I ask them to clarify what this actually means. If something in the working relationship called for them to choose between dinner at home and achieving a work demand, which would take priority? If their priority doesn't match with the other party's expectations, this is important information for everyone to discuss, clarify, and try to find a way to harmonize—perhaps using the "five whys" method.

Evaluating the Touchstone

Vision, Mission, Values & Principles, and Constraints & Imperatives are the four elements that form the Touchstone.

---

[11] "We need to establish shared standards that allow us to work together in harmony. This can be tremendously enriching, but it is also extremely difficult. Unfortunately, many of us settle for pseudo-harmony rather than facing the hard work of creating the real thing. The desire to keep the (semblance of) peace often leads us to avoid conflict, sweeping our differences under the carpet. Unaddressed, these disagreements turn into contempt, resentment, and mistrust." *Conscious Business, supra* p.180.

Always keep in mind the purpose of the Touchstone. It is intended to function in the context of the parties' relationship, guiding actions in times of accord as well as supporting productive conflict resolution. The Touchstone will form the basis for evaluating the acceptability of the parties' decisions and plans (for each individual party and for their constituents) as the relationship and endeavor go forward.

Even with the best intentions, our sense of fairness is easily tainted by self-interest. When we have a gut reaction to something, we are all too easily persuaded that our immediate response arising from that gut reaction is appropriate, reasonable, and understandable. It is true that gut reactions provide important information, but they can lead us to hasty action that we later regret, or trigger an escalation of combativeness in our conflict partners. The Touchstone should provide a robust reminder of what *really* matters—how the parties would like to behave—to recall them to their deeply held values and visions and keep them on track to accomplishing the well-articulated and delineated mission. The Touchstone comprises their criteria for decision making, reminders of what really matters (for when they are distracted by emotional or conditioned responses to events), and the rationale behind the contractual deal points, terms, and conditions.

By sharing Touchstones in the context of drafting an agreement, parties have a chance to check that what is driving the other's decisions is in alignment with their own criteria. And isn't it great to know that at the outset rather than discovering that as they go along? If they've had that kind of conversation before they get to the deal points—or in tandem with the discussion of the deal points—what they've done is formed a relationship that tells them whether they have a good fit, and it establishes a connection that is far more meaningful and viable than what we tend to get when we just haggle over the deal points.

With the conventional approach, a relationship is formed, but it is an adversarial relationship based on how the parties are interpreting each other's behavior relying largely on guesswork. By contrast, when we begin to discover where we are in agreement and talk things through, we are forming a relationship based on mutual comprehension of one another that we've confirmed by having the conversation. We're not interpreting, we're not guessing—we've actually had a conversation that is robust enough that we know what's up with ourselves and the other party.

This is a much healthier way to enter a relationship than if one or both parties feel that they've got some kind of score to settle or that they've been taken advantage of during the drafting of the contract.

For lawyer and client, beyond its usefulness in the context of contract formation and performance, the Touchstone has additional value. With a firm grasp on what really matters—what are their key values, guiding principles, and constraints and imperatives—the client will find it easier to stay in their own integrity if they are drawn against their will into the coercive forum of our legal justice system; and the lawyer will be better equipped to provide useful counsel about options as they arise. Sometimes, litigation is unavoidable. There are those who use litigation to intimidate—so-called "trolls."[12] There are those who truly believe they have been wronged and that the conventional system is the best way to address the wrong, the harm they are experiencing. If one knows what one's personal integrity and the company's integrity (bottom line) are, then that knowledge becomes a touchstone for evaluating the array of choices that present themselves throughout the coercive conflict process should that become necessary.

---

[12] "Troll" is a term often used to indicate a party who demonstrates a pattern of instigating lawsuits in order to trigger their targets to settle the claims for nuisance value (something less than defense of the suit is likely to cost).

CHAPTER 6

Addressing Change & Engaging Disagreement Structure and System

The parties to a contract have come together to cooperate, but there are natural, sometimes disruptive, tensions between what is good for one and what is good for the unit. It is unsurprising that the Prisoner's Dilemma is a staple of research dealing with relationship dynamics. This research, as we have seen, demonstrates that the way the conversation is framed exerts a strong influence over how participants respond to dilemma.[1] The experience of the Touchstone conversation combined with the resulting written statement provides an intentional contextual frame for the parties' conflict conversation.

The system that the parties use to engage in conflict also has a strong influence on how they respond to one another and the situation. The default system is our conventional legal process, which is designed for adversarial conflict and encourages—even incentivizes—combativeness, intimidation, and zero-sum thinking. Conventional contracts are written with this system of adversarial conflict in mind.

Discovering Agreement (DA) addresses the needs of conflict, but does not assume that the default system is the only option. If the parties are not happy with the way the conventional system

---

[1] *The Name of the Game,* Liberman *supra.*

impacts their choices and relationship, they do not have to acquiesce. Using the "private law" of their contract, they can design their own proprietary justice system. Rather than adopt the traditional approaches of bygone contracts, the parties can use the contract language to recast conflict and dispute between themselves as a nonadversarial, cocreative undertaking. This begins with the Touchstone conversation when the parties share and comprehend the meaning of their relationship and work for themselves, their constituents and the larger world.

I have learned from harsh experience, however, that having only a generalized promise to keep conflict conversations nonadversarial and focused on returning to alignment with the Touchstone is insufficient to break our long-practiced habits or the grip of emotion when faced with the turmoil that accompanies conflict. When anger or distress erupts for one or both parties, it is remarkably difficult to interrupt the flow between that stimulus and the conditioned reactions to conflict. With their emotional alarms sounding, the parties' first impulse is not to come together for an empathic, compassionate exchange, no matter what their early intentions may have been. To the contrary, they tend to look for and rapidly implement unilateral solutions that they feel serve their needs, often precipitating the dissolution of the relationship.

To increase the chances that they will be able to conduct their conflict as partners rather than opponents, parties need systemic and structural support that evokes and encourages cooperation and collaboration. Interruption between stimulus and response is crucial. Parties are much more likely to be able to make a conscious, considered response to disruption if, before the emotional stimulus of conflict ever occurs, they have in place a structural system that receives the stimulus and channels the energy it generates in a more productive direction. Having to work their way through a process of structured, organized response to the stimulus breaks the momentum of simplistic, emotionally driven reactions and makes space for considered and optimized problem-solving responses. The "dispute resolution" provisions of the contract are an ideal place to embed these supportive systems and procedures.

Setting the Frame and Framework for Productive Conflict

Using provisions I call, "Addressing Change and Engaging Disagreement" (ACED) the parties set in place a structure and procedure designed to focus and channel the energy of conflict and dispute toward collaborative problem solving and creativity.

It is often said conflict indicates a disconnection, but in reality, apathy indicates disconnection. By contrast, conflict is actually a signal that there is a meaningful connection between the parties, and something important has changed. Their connection has become uncomfortable and is causing friction. They can either try to break the connection or they can work together to upgrade it.

There are three key aspects of conflict that the structure must address. Firstly, there is the harm that gives rise to the conflict. One party to the contract (or possibly both) is no longer satisfied with the way things are going. There is some important interest or need that is no longer being met, and it is urgent enough to draw focused energy and attention. Secondly, there are the emotions that accompany dispute. Emotions arise and are expressed most often as anger and indignation. The usual adversarial response to these emotions and unmet needs is to look for who is at fault, who should bear the blame, who should be "held accountable." Which brings us to the third aspect of conflict that the structure must address—finding a way back to harmony.

Trying to end the conflict by imposing conventional accountability—with its economic/financial connotation—generally means deciding who has to pay (and how much) in order to satisfy the suffering party that accounts are back in balance. While there are times when someone's actions have created harm and making amends is appropriate or even imperative, for the most part, imposing conventional accountability will not restore harmony or satisfy the true, underlying needs of either party. It usually triggers a contest to assign blame, leading to a destructive spiral of tit-for-tat accusations and demands.

Lasting and satisfying resolution is rarely the result of "putting things back the way they were" or "evening the score." Durable, meaningful resolution is far more likely to be achieved by fixing the problem the parties are faced with in the present moment and addressing the conditions that gave rise to it (so it doesn't happen again). What is actually more productive than bickering over who is in the most pain and who should wear the black hat, is redirecting the exploration towards finding what has changed, establishing mutual comprehension of the meaning of the new situation for all involved, and collaborating to make the adjustments that will get things back on a productive, beneficial course for everyone as quickly as possible.

This involves a fundamental shift away from an adversarial operational logic of enforcement; retribution; and coercion towards a logic of restored cooperation, productivity, and mutuality. The goal is to optimize the creative potential inherent in conflict and minimize the tendency to adopt destructive patterns, responses, and positions.

There are myriad books, articles, and conflict professionals available that outline and teach the principles of nonadversarial conflict.[2] These resources offer particular (and varying)

---

[2] Friedman, Gary J., and Jack Himmelstein. *Challenging Conflict: Mediation through Understanding.* Chicago, IL: American Bar Association, 2008. Print.; Levine, Stewart. *Getting to Resolution: Turning Conflict into Collaboration.* San Francisco, CA: Berrett-Koehler, 2009. Print.; Mnookin, Robert H., Scott R. Peppet, and Andrew S. Tulumello. *Beyond Winning: Negotiating to Create Value in Deals and Disputes.* Cambridge, MA: Belknap of Harvard UP, 2000. Print.; Pranis, Kay. *The Little Book of Circle Processes: A New/Old Approach to Peacemaking.* Intercourse, PA: Good, 2005. Print.; Ury, William. *The Power*

preexisting procedures and structures. DA parties can adopt or adapt one or more of these preexisting structures, or they can design their own from scratch. Whether the parties intend to adopt, adapt, or create their own process for conducting productive conflict, when drafting the ACED structure and procedure, it is important to remain aware of key principles and elements that longtime practitioners find are the essential to successfully interrupting habitual adversarial patterns and redirecting attention and energy towards nonadversarial, cocreative conflict.

These key elements are:

- Having the system in place prior to conflict
- Having a system designed by the parties that will use it
- Orienting and integrating the chosen system within the broader, existing power structures of the community at large

The system should include specific steps and procedures that help the parties:

- Interrupt habitual reactivity
- Close the distance that conflict has opened between them
- Reorient their conflict conversation towards collaboration

It should also include a structural framework that supports meaningful dialogue, including:

- Gaining mutual comprehension
- Taking responsibility

---

of a Positive No: How to Say No and Still Get to Yes. New York: Bantam, 2007. Print.; Ury, William, Jeanne M. Brett, and Stephen B. Goldberg. *Getting Disputes Resolved: Designing Systems to Cut the Costs of Conflict.* San Francisco: Jossey-Bass, 1988. Print. – to name just a few.

- Cocreating a plan for moving forward that works for everyone
- Developing specific steps for following up and assessing the efficacy of the plan/resolution

Have the System in Place before Dispute Erupts

It is notoriously difficult to bring parties to alternative dispute resolution after dispute has erupted.[3] Experience demonstrates it is much more difficult to shift away from established, habitual conflict patterns if the shift is attempted after conflict is already heated. For this reason, it is important to have a clear, visible, easily accessible system in place before dispute arises. Clear means that the conversational structure is described in a way all parties can understand. Visible means the community knows about and is aware of the alternative conflict system and the description is in a place where it can be easily found and referenced by participants before and during the conflict conversation. Accessible means that anyone in the community (either party) can initiate a conflict conversation without having to get approval or permission from any gatekeepers.

Community Created[4]

Prescribing a procedure for a community is less effective than facilitating the community in designing its own system for engaging conflict productively. The particular culture of the community strongly affects what makes sense—what will

---

[3] De Vries, Berend R., and Maurits Barendrecht. "Fitting the Forum to the Fuss with Sticky Defaults: Failure in the Market for Dispute Resolution Services?" Cardozo *Journal of Conflict Resolution* 7.1 (2006), Available at SSRN: http://ssrn.com/abstract=811244 or DOI: 10.2139/ssrn.572042.

[4] In the case of a contract, the parties and their constituents comprise the community.

escalate conflict or inspire peacemaking.[5] What is more, when the community creates its own system, community members are more invested in using their improved system and in seeing it succeed. This "buy-in" is a key factor in the successful implementation of the system.

The more the parties are clear ahead of time about why they want an alternative dispute resolution structure (why it is good for them and their success) and what the precise steps are to initiate and engage in the nonadversarial, cocreative process, the better their chances of averting harmful and destructive reactivity, and the more likely it is they will be able to come together and take advantage of the creative potential inherent in all conflict. They are ready to problem-solve and upgrade or transform their relationship rather than flinging accusations, destroy ing the trust and sacrificing the beneficial purpose they formerly shared. Designing an intentional, improved response to disruption within a relationship means taking a conscious look at what works and what doesn't work for these particular parties.

Helpful questions to explore include:

- In your experience, what sort of actions or practices have worked well to calm things down and open lines of communication?
- What sorts of things have had the opposite effect?
- What things have worked against your being able to come together and have a productive conversation with some who is angry?
- What tends to escalate anger or misunderstanding?
- What have you found promotes mutual understanding and cooperation?

---

[5] Yazzie, The Honorable Robert. "Life Comes from It: Navajo Justice Concepts." *New Mexico Law Review* Spring, p.24 (1994): 175; Sklar, Charlotte. "Alternative Courts in Tribal Communities." *2d Annual Peacemakers Gathering: Preserving Tribal Justice through Indigenous Peacemaking, Executive Summary* (2008): Appendix.

Within the context of the answers to these questions, the next step is to explore:

- What are our key values for how conflict should be engaged between us?
- What would that look like in practice?
- How would that function?
- What resources will we need to make this work? (where will we meet, do we want/need to have designated facilitators)
- How will we evaluate the effectiveness of our conflict conversations?

It is important to remember the pitfalls of creating rules and incentives. In creating the ACED system to support cocreative responses to difficult situations, we want to minimize the tendency to devolve into arguing about how rules should be interpreted and whether one or the other party is adequately following the rules for engaging conflict. This is not a place where sanctions and deterrents are helpful.

My experience is that setting their Touchstone as a frame for the conversation—as a focal point to remind the parties of the values they want to honor as they engage in the conflict conversation—and then creating a roadmap with key steps and questions the parties will use to enter the conversation, explore their situation, and design their own resolutions provides enough structure while also allowing for the flexibility that real-life demands. As they put the system to work, the parties can tweak the details—keeping what works and changing what they learn is counterproductive to their practice of nonadversarial, cocreative conflict.

Interrupting Habitual Reactivity: Counteracting "Automatic Pilot"

Conflict is a natural part of every relationship. Yet, conflict feels dangerous because we tend to understand it as putting us in opposition to others—needing to protect and defend our interests against an adversary. Our comfort and safety are threatened, and threats trigger our limbic responses. In the context of contractual relationships, our limbic "fight/ flight/freeze" response tends to be cloaked in more acceptable "civilized" expressions such as assigning blame or characterizing the other party as wrong, idiotic, or selfish. We often will try to distance ourselves from one another or the situation by ignoring or avoiding discussion.

When our limbic danger-response is activated, it has a powerful impact on our mental and emotional capacities; we do not have access to our full intelligence, our full creativity, nor our full capacity for compassion.[6] Decisions made and actions taken in this state tend to be automatic rather than considered, and knee-jerk reactions often create results that are less than optimum. Because most people's automatic response to conflict is to expect and bring a fight, the first essential element for supporting productive conflict is a mechanism that interrupts the chain of adversarial reactivity. When conflict triggers the fight/flight/freeze response, we need something that takes us off automatic pilot and puts the controls back in manual mode. The ACED provisions help do this by providing a specific and predetermined procedure that the parties agree to follow to initiate their conflict conversations.

Shifting from Debate to Dialogue

> *The problem of cooperation, then, is getting collective*

---

[6] Goleman, Daniel. *Emotional Intelligence: Why It Can Matter More than IQ: & Working with Emotional Intelligence.* London: Bloomsbury, 2004. Print.

interest to triumph over individual interest, when possible.

—*Joshua Greene, Moral Tribes*

Productive conflict requires creating and cultivating the conditions for meaningful dialogue between the parties. In the often referenced "tragedy of the commons" scenario (where individuals acting independently based on "rational self-interest" deplete some common resource), selfishness threatens cooperation. Contracts are meant to help parties productively manage the natural Me versus Us tensions that arise in any relationship, but sometimes tensions become overwhelming causing the parties to no longer see themselves as sharing a purpose and interests. They slip into conventional mindsets and the choice each faces appears to be Us versus Them. It is when one or both parties are caught up in an adversarial perspective that the importance of frame and framework is demonstrated. The Touchstone and ACED provisions embody the parties' codesigned structure and system for how they will respond to disruptive change and obdurate conflict amongst themselves.

Frame

For DA parties, the written Touchstone is a unified expression of what really matters. It provides a shared metric for weighing options, even in the midst of Us versus Them reactivity. When a conflict arises between parties, rather than trying to jump directly into a conversation about what happened to cause the conflict, the Touchstone first grounds their conversation by reminding the parties of their common currency and the good reasons they each have for engaging in their chosen, nonadversarial process. In essence, the Touchstone statement recalls for them what they were aiming at when they began, and what are the values and principles they have chosen as their guides. From there, they can more readily discuss the new situation in which they find themselves and what sort of course corrections make the most sense in the context of Touchstone. Their conversation is no longer rooted in assigning blame; rather, it is about recalibrating alignment of their actions with their deeply held values in their shared effort to accomplish their key mission and serve their vision of a better world.

Framework

Although the Touchstone and a commitment to productive conflict can often be enough to reorient the parties' conversation towards productive collaboration, difficult situations and the heightened emotions that accompany conflict can require additional support to avert escalating hostilities. It is wise to be prepared for more difficult and potentially intractable disagreements. Mediators and others who facilitate collaborative, nonadversarial conflict know it can be crucial to have an agreed process, a structure for conducting conversations that supports meaningful dialogue—opening the lines of communication, restoring and sustaining everyone's capacity to hear and understand one another, and counteracting the inclination to harden positions.

It would be ideal if we could rely on the parties to turn immediately to the Touchstone when conflict or crisis erupts, but we know from experience that when emotion is heightened, it is far more likely that habitual conflict patterns will be followed. Blame will be thrown and the attack/ counterattack spiral commenced. Thus, to ensure that the parties do indeed take advantage of their well-considered Touchstone, it is important to have in place a structure, a contractually agreed mechanism that supports—even requires—them to notice when they are caught in a chain of reactivity and find that still point, to take the pause and reconnect with their highest intentions.

Closing the Distance: Have a Way to "Walk Toward Conflict"

It is natural to want to put distance between ourselves and the painful sensations of anger, fear, and hurt that accompany conflict. Most of us find it counterintuitive to expect people to come together and cooperate with the person/s they see as the source of their unhappiness. However, experienced facilitators of productive conflict agree that closing the distance is key.

Dominic Barter, speaking about his work facilitating restorative conflict, describes an early epiphany. He was riding his bike in Amsterdam, and a couple holding a heated conversation stood blocking his path. Dom stopped a little distance away. As he waited and watched, he witnessed the couple repeating themselves, saying the same things over and over while raising their voices louder and louder. It is understandable for people to raise their voices to be heard when physical distance between them increases; but here, the pair were still physically very close to one another, close enough to be heard without shouting. So, why were they shouting? It seemed to Dominic that there was a strong correlation between the increasing volume and each person's belief that their partner was not hearing or understanding them. They were trying to close the perceived distance by shouting—raising the volume.[7]

When we have a problem that we cannot resolve on our own, we want others to hear, understand, and help us fix it. If we do not get the attention, understanding, and assistance that we need, we will raise the volume. Volume can be raised with voices or with actions, and raised volume indicates an increasing distance—lack of understanding—between the parties. One lesson that productive conflict experts have learned is that the way to lower the volume of a conflict is to help the parties close

---

[7] Barter, Dominic. "DominicBarterJune12015." *SoundCloud.* Keynote Address, Nat'l Assoc. of Community and Restorative Justice, 1 June 2015. Web. 25 Aug. 2015.

the distance—to listen and to understand one another. Dominic calls it "walking towards conflict." J. Kim Wright[8] gives similar advice:

> *I've found that the best thing to do in conflict is the very thing that is counter-intuitive. Just as we want to get away from each other, we especially need to come together and sort it out. The longer a conflict goes without intervention, the worse it tends to get. We make up our story about why we are justified in our position, we collect evidence, either from our own minds or from others. Often we call the people most likely to support us in the story we have. For example, I wouldn't tend to call a friend of my ex to talk about how horrible he is. I'd call someone who already doesn't like him. Sometimes calling a few people can convince me that I am totally right and he is a bigger jerk than I ever imagined. Everything I ever liked about him disappears. This is a pretty typical human response that continues unless interrupted.*

The ACED supports the parties in coming together and lowering the volume, so that the energy of conflict can be harnessed to improve rather than harm their relationship.

Designing or Choosing a Structure and Procedure

The first essential step for any justice system is having a way for the community to access and initiate a conflict conversation. Lawyers know where to find the Rules of Procedure and what

---

[8] Wright, J. Kim. *Lawyers as Peacemakers: Practicing Holistic, Problem-solving Law.* Chicago, IL: American Bar Association, 2010. Print.; www.cuttingedgelaw.com.

the steps are for initiating a formal adversarial conflict proceeding. The ACED should provide the parties with their own process for calling and preparing for a cocreative conversation. The parties will need to know: what is the button we push, the number we call, or the e-mail form we use in order to start the process? If it is an e-mail message, who should it be addressed to and what should be included in the content? Is there a key subject line that should be used so that everyone knows this is a message about addressing a rising tension or closing a widening distance?

Make sure there are clear and easy steps that any/all parties can take at their own discretion to initiate a cocreative conflict conversation. The initiation trigger should be readily available and easy to use. Ideally, it will involve minimal hoops to jump through and be free of requiring the approval or permission of any gatekeepers before the conversation process can be started. In terms of practicalities, the whole process is much more likely to move forward smoothly if there is already agreement about where cocreative conversations will be held, what other resources need to be available (white board and markers? designated/trained facilitator?) and what is the process for deciding who will be invited to participate in the conversation.

Another step is establishing how the parties want to prepare for the conversation. Keep in mind that one of the functions of the system is to help the parties switch tracks from high-speed, habitual reactivity and adversarial positioning to a more measured, considered train of thought where they reconnect with their core vision, values, and mission before evaluating options or making decisions.

It may be helpful for the parties or their designated conversation facilitator to go through preassigned steps such as:

- Rereading the Touchstone statement
- Reading a statement (contained the ACED provisions) that reminds them of why they have chosen to create and

follow their own system for engaging conflict
- Exchanging lists of who each party believes needs to be present to maximize the productivity of the cocreative conversation

Sometimes an individual will not want to participate. If this happens there can be a strong temptation for the other individuals to veer into an adversarial response to this unwillingness, believing that the person should be coerced into attending. The key—as always—is to interrupt "automatic pilot" responses, step back, slow down, and shift into manual mode. One of the parties or the community's designated facilitator might reach out to the reluctant attendee and explore what is the concern that causes them to refuse participation. Every invitee should know that they are asked to join the conversation as a valued participant whose perspective, knowledge, and support is considered essential to creating a plan that will work for everyone. These are moments when that Touchstone and the statement in the ACED about why the parties' system is preferred over the alternative, conventional conflict models can be very helpful.

The final step for initiating the conversation is to set the time and make sure that everyone who has been identified as essential to the conversation has been invited.

The Conversational Roadmap

In addition to including in the contract the practical elements of the parties' system, the ACED provisions should describe a structure for conducting the conversation that evokes and supports meaningful dialogue. Debate is the conversational logic of litigation, engaged to persuade a third party. Dialogue, by contrast, is not about persuasion. It is carried on between the conflict conversation participants to gather information and increase mutual understanding.

Defining the ideal is one thing. Engaging in real-life dialogue usually requires some structural support. Meaningful dialogue includes a particular quality of listening. In meaningful dialogue, listening is not just a job of the listener, it is something that happens amongst and between people who are working together to gain mutual comprehension— to confirm that the message the speaker wants to convey matches the message that the listener/s have understood. There are many versions of such listening structures that are designed to encourage and support parties not necessarily disposed to openness and dialogue to engage in this particular quality of communication.

Key Components of Meaningful Dialogue

Mutual Comprehension

Mutual comprehension processes—sometimes called, "perspective-taking" by neuroscience researchers[9]—seem most effective when they include what Gary Friedman calls "looping,"[10] what Stephen R. Covey calls an "empathy loop,"[11] and others identify as "reflective listening."[12] In all of these conversational structures the listener's job is not to listen in order to rebut or respond; the listener's job is to listen in order to understand what the speaker is trying to communicate. It is a collaborative activity between listener and speaker in that part of this listening requires the listener to tell the speaker what they believe the speaker intends them to understand. In essence, the listener

---

[9] Lamm, Claus, C. Daniel Batson, and Jean Decety. "The Neural Substrate of Human Empathy: Effects of Perspective-taking and Cognitive Appraisal." *Journal of Cognitive Neuroscience* 19.1 (2007): 42–58. Web.

[10] Friedman, *Challenging Conflict, supra,* Chapter 4.

[11] Covey, Stephen R., and Breck England. *The 3rd Alternative: Solving Life's Most Difficult Problems.* New York: Free Press, 2011. Print.

[12] Arnold, Kyle. "Posts." *Reflective Listening: Rogers' Paradox.* Saybrook University, 4 June 2015. Web. 28 Aug. 2015.

expresses in their own words the message that they believe the speaker is trying to convey—without expressing an opinion or offering a rebuttal. The speaker then either confirms that listener has understood correctly (accurately and completely) or will try again to explain what is important for the listener to understand. This cyclical process is repeated until the speaker can confirm for the listener that they have accurately and completely understood the message the speaker is trying to impart.

Self-responsibility

> *You must take unconditional responsibility; you need to see yourself as a "player," as a central character who has contributed to shape the current situation— and who can thus affect the future. This is the opposite of seeing yourself as a "victim" subject to forces beyond your control. The player is in the game and can affect the result. The victim is out of the game and can only suffer the consequences of others' actions.*
>
> *—Fred Kofman, Conscious Business*

"Victimhood" is a state where one is (or feels) powerless to affect one's own well-being or to prevent a harm or take self-preserving action.[13] In adversarial conflict, victimhood can become a prized position. Having been powerless in the face of a wrongdoer absolves the victim of responsibility. In the adversarial contest for the favor of a third-party adjudicator, laying blame and shifting responsibility for events and harms is an inevitable part of the process. Holding someone accountable in the context of adversarial conflict means shifting the burden of loss in an attempt to even a score by making the losing party pay. In a nonadversarial, cocreative conflict, the reason to review

---

[13] Dominic Barter has said, "Victimhood is when the power to affect my well-being feels as if it is out of my reach."

what happened in the past is not so that a loser will be determined and punished. Exploring what happened in the past is done so that the parties can understand the conditions that existed and gave rise to the problem or harmful event, so that they can make the changes that will prevent the recurrence of the problem and harm, and so the ones affected by the event can decide how best to address the resultant harm. In nonadversarial conflict "victimhood" has no value. All parties are there as powerful players, joining forces to solve problems, transform conditions, and create a world that works for everyone.

Because habits of victimhood and blame-throwing are hard to shake, parties to a cocreative conflict conversation may find it helpful to include a process for reorienting exploration of "what happened" away from blame-throwing and towards gathering important information for problem solving and improved future planning. Accepting responsibility is important, but finding out which and whose actions created the harm is only part of the inquiry. The rest of the inquiry is to discover why those actions were taken—what good reason did the party have for making that choice? That motivation, the need that was being served, is important information. It will need to be considered when the parties design their plans for going forward.

Some ways of doing this include, each party being asked to explain the action and its consequences from the other party's perspective, or answering the question, "Can you say why that action might have seemed like a good idea for the other party?" Another way to approach this is for the parties to explore the problem from a series of distinct and limited perspectives by asking and answering questions such as:

- What are the facts—not our evaluation of them, just the bare, observable facts?
- What about the resulting situation in which we find ourselves is actually a positive, an actual or potential benefit?

- What are the problems or concerns inherent in this situation?
- What is my/your gut reaction, emotional response to the situation?
- What new ideas does this situation trigger?

The process of taking turns answering "perspective specific" questions and/or explaining what one thinks the other party's viewpoint might be, helps shift the parties from "you're the problem" thinking to "we have a problem" perspectives. This, combined with a confirmed understanding of what really matters to each party in the given situation (gained from the "mutual comprehension" process), provides a sturdy platform from which the parties can codesign their action plan for going forward. They now know one another's needs, intentions, concerns, and interests and they have a better grasp of what is at the root of their respective actions. They also have a much clearer sense of the parameters of the problem they face and the destination they would like to design a path to reach.

It is at this point that they can move into making proposals based on serving all the needs that have been put on the table. They can turn to getting answers to questions such as:

- What do we want to happen next?
- What information do we need to gather?
- What information are we going to have to assume?
- Given all we now know and what we see is important to each of us—and given the Touchstone—what is our best plan that we can design?

Mechanism to Assess Efficacy—Follow-up/Check-in

The ACED can also have a reminder that any resolution action plan should include a set time and place for the parties to reconvene and either celebrate the success of the resolution, tweak the plan to make it better, or engage a renewed exploration of the needs that remain unmet so a new and improved solution can be codesigned.

Moving Successfully through Conflict

With the Touchstone and ACED provisions, the parties create for themselves a structure that has the capacity to engage the full spectrum of emotion inherent in conflict and enable a rational response made with integrity, and focused on productive action. By making the commitment—before conflict arises—that they will engage conflict collaboratively, and use it as an opportunity to make course corrections that work for everyone and that bring them back into alignment with their Touchstone, the parties reframe the purpose and norms of conflict within their relationship.

With the Touchstone already in place, they have their agreed context and criteria—the specifications for designing upgrades and improvements, bug-fixes and course corrections for their coendeavor. By adding—and linking to the Touchstone—a preagreed procedure for initiating and conducting nonadversarial, cocreative conflict, the parties short-circuit the habitual, destructive patterns that tend to drag dispute into a downward spiral. And, by making participation in their proprietary process a contractual precondition to engaging adversarial procedures, the parties integrate their system into the larger, conventional power structure of the existing legal system.

Setting the conflict conversation's focus on the Touchstone and channeling attention and effort toward designing a solution that aligns with their acknowledged vision, mission, and values, shifts the parties out of automatic "toe-to-toe" argumentative postures and into "side-by-side" intentional exploration and brainstorming. Their conversation is not a backward-looking effort to shift blame. Rather than trading accusations, attacking and counterattacking one another, they are—together—asking themselves, "What were we aiming for? Where are we now? How do we get back on track?" The capacity to shift from an adversarial to a collaborative response in the midst of conflict is genuine bargaining power.

Sometimes, a simple rereading of their Touchstone statement/s can help clarify for one or both parties the point of misalignment between what they intended or expected and the actions being taken or proposed. In this way, by orienting to the Touchstone, the parties shift to a conversation that is not about who is right or wrong but about checking alignment—noting where things appear to one party to be out of alignment, and allowing the other party to give a perspective on why the action in question does align. This is a very different conversation than the search to assign blame and fault.

> *What is important is that the person's thoughts, feelings, or actions are recognized and acknowledged. Plain and simple.*
> —Roger Fisher and Daniel Shapiro, Beyond Reason

Having the Touchstone helps each party understand, acknowledge and find merit in the other party's reasoning. They can say, "I see where you are coming from," without agreeing with the other's conclusions or accepting their proposed strategy. This helps keep lines of communications open and provides useful information when a party is trying to form an alternative proposal that will meet everyone's needs. Offering a proposal designed to meet the other party's needs makes the proposal more "reasonable."

A Contract That Learns

In his foreword to Fred Kofman's book, *Conscious Business*, Peter Senge exhorts us to consider which is more valuable—knowing or learning.[14] In the fast-paced, disruptive, digital marketplace, "knowing" is ephemeral. Learning supports adaptability which nurtures success in an ever-changing world. What could be better than a contract that has the capacity to learn along with the parties?

Because conflicts are engaged within a cooperative system designed to reconnect and realign with the Touchstone, there is room for embracing shifts in priorities as well as changes in vision, mission, and even values. The ACED conversational structure begins with examining together the declared Touchstone—the parties' Vision, Mission, Values & Principles, and Constraints & Imperatives—and then exploring for what is true for each party in the present moment. This review may remind them of what actually does matter, or it could make clear that something key is missing from their original Touchstone statement and needs to be added to the overall conversation.

The point is not so much to assure that everyone stays bound to the declared Vision, Mission, and Values embodied in the Touchstone but to assure that there is a way to discover if the Touchstone is still accurate and complete. Remember, looking *at* the frame is the first step—both to remind the parties what they intended to be their guiding principles and to verify that the frame as defined in their original Touchstone is still accurate and relevant. If it is not, the ACED structure and the questions they are asking and answering together, provide a process for discovering the new and improved Touchstone, and for the cocreation of a new action plan that works for all.

The ACED commitment is to allowing the structure to provide the navigational system by which they explore the new

---

[14] *Conscious Business, supra* Foreword.; Peter M. Senge. Society for Organizational Learning, North America, Web. 28 Aug. 2015.; Senge, Peter M. *The Fifth Discipline: The Art and Practice of the Learning Organization.* New York: Doubleday/Currency, 2006. Print.

territory that conflict has opened for their relationship and endeavor. The questions and process are designed to support the parties in optimizing their ability to imagine possibilities and make wise, well-considered plans for their respective and shared futures.

Having Backup Procedures and Support

There may be times when the parties cannot recover agreement on their own. For this reason, it is wise for them to also choose and include in the contract a "backup" structure for a supervised/facilitated conversation. There are several restorative structures/models available for dispute resolution that have been practiced for decades and have established track records for success. These include interest-based negotiations,[15] joint-session mediation,[16] and circle processes.[17] Although it is generally not possible to contract away one's right to litigate, the parties can make the restorative, nonadversarial approach a precondition to initiating adversarial proceedings. Doing this gives them a real and meaningful chance to enter a creative rather than destructive spiral.

Litigation Is Always an Option

Having these mechanisms is not a magical solution, nor is it a promise that conflict will never arise or never be painful. Discovering Agreement is not an automated system that acts on

---

[15] Fisher, Roger, and William Ury. *Getting to Yes: Negotiating an Agreement without Giving in.* London: Random House Business, 2012. Print.

[16] Chrisman, P. Oswin, Gay G. Cox, and Petra Novotna. "Collaborative Practice Mediation: Are We Ready to Serve This Emerging Market." *Pepperdine Dispute Resolution Law Journal* 6.3 (2006): 451–64. Web. 28 Aug. 2015. Available at: http://digitalcommons.pepperdine.edu/drlj/vol6/iss3/4.

[17] Pranis, Kay. *The Little Book of Circle Processes: A New/Old Approach to Peacemaking.* Intercourse, PA: Good, 2005. Print.

the parties. It is a hand-operated frame and framework that the parties can use to orient and organize their cooperative response to conflict. They may not be able to prevent litigation. Old habits and attitudes can be remarkably difficult to shed, and this is especially true when one is in the throes of heated disagreement or crisis.

Often I'm asked the "what if " questions—What if one party won't participate in the process? What if one party lies about their Values or Vision? These are not questions that exist only in the context of a DA conversation and contract. What DA offers is a greater chance that change and conflict can be engaged productively and fundamental differences can be revealed and reconciled or, if not reconciled, the parties can know sooner rather than later that the relationship has a significant misalignment to contend with. The condition precedent that the parties must engage in the ACED process before initiating adversarial process provides a certain diversionary power, but if a party is truly determined to engage coercive, adversarial proceedings, they will likely be able to force it to happen at some point. It is important to remember, however, that the conventional, coercive system is there even more immediately for parties who have not created for themselves a systemic structure and support for Discovering Agreement.

CHAPTER 7

Lawyers and Clients

In my experience, a fundamental belief held by attorneys and parties to a negotiation is that *dominance equals power*, and one needs this domination power to achieve safety, certainty, predictability, and to gain for oneself the maximum benefit from the contractual relationship. It is believed that, to achieve dominance, one has to be able to control things, to persuade and, if that fails, force the other party to accept one's choices. A domination power dynamic places the parties on opposite sides of the table and characterizes their interests as adverse. Corollaries to having adverse interests include the imperative that each side should and shall try to take advantage of the other, and the more paranoid and the bigger a bully one is, the more likely one is to get the optimum outcome for oneself.

Holding this perspective means that we must seek to gain power by developing a set of tools and capacities that give us an advantage over others in games of coercion. According to this logic of relational power, certain "power tools" (i.e., money, political status, skin color, social standing, media access, education) are imperative. In order to get along, to get ahead, to stay safe, and to get a fair share, many of us believe we must use these tools to our advantage in a constant competition for control of limited resources and returns. When we believe we must compete for power, "power" becomes a euphemism for dominance, and "justice" becomes a euphemism for coercion and retribution.

When the underlying assumption is that the power to make ourselves safe derives from the ability to coerce others, then achieving safety requires reliance on enforcement by governmental authority. To coerce someone, we need to be able to call upon powers of governmental might (courts and police power). The ability to do this largely depends upon one's having access to money, status, and political power. All of these power sources have gatekeepers. If you want to acquire coercion via one or more, you will need to curry the favor of, persuade, or become the gatekeeper. Gatekeeper power sources are not wholly reliable. Money, status, and political power can all be lost or taken. We cannot truly control the outcomes of coercive processes, as anyone who has ever engaged in litigation can attest.

This profound realization generates the search for a power source that has no gatekeeper. This search leads to those who have wielded great power without having access to the sources of dominant, coercive strength—Gandhi, Dr. Martin Luther King, Jr., and Nelson Mandela, among many others. All of them have in common a nonadversarial perspective. They each grounded their actions in, and demonstrated the truth of, their certainty that nonviolence is far more powerful than violence in bringing an end to harms and creating lasting resolution of conflict.[1] The foundation of their nonviolent activism was the practice of satyagraha— Gandhi's word meaning "holding tight to truth."

Knowing one's truth—what really matters—and consciously aligning one's actions with those deeply held values is the ultimate power source. This is integrity. Integrity is the

---

[1] Gandhi saw "ahimsa" (literally "no injury") as the most effective principle for social action because of humankind's innate desire for peace, justice, and personal dignity. Where violence meets force with force, nonviolence transforms relationships to bring about peaceful resolution to conflict and dispute. *Gandhi on Nonviolence, supra,* p.35.; As Dominic Barter has expressed it, "I can take care of myself without harming others; and I can take care of others without harming myself."

fundamental pillar of credibility and trust. Trust and trustworthiness is a powerful force much greater and more durable than dominance. Personal integrity is the one thing in this world that a person has total control of. You can sell it, give it away, or betray it, but no one can take from you your personal integrity.[2]

The Touchstone is, essentially, the statement of a person's or a group's "truth," and having a clear, ready expression of that truth helps the people involved hold to that truth when emotion and crisis would pressure them to abandon their core principles. Companies and organizations in the 21st century are increasingly aware of the impact of reputation and perceived disintegrity in a world with instantaneous, digital communications. Conscious integration of corporate values into the life of a company—its interactions with the community and within its own internal culture—has been found to have an overriding importance to a company's long-term success.[3]

Corporate integrity involves stating the deeply held values that serve as guiding principles and integrating those into the fabric of the business by putting in place systemic decision-making and problem-solving processes that support employees in acting beyond mere compliance with laws and regulations, infusing their work and the overall enterprise with meaningful purpose beyond profit and growth.

When the company knows what really matters, and has expressed it in written form, they have a lodestar available to keep them oriented. For example, if a company is clear and has a ready reminder that what really matters to them is making a profit while having zero negative impact on the natural

---

[2] "Everything can be taken from a man but one thing: the last of the human freedoms—to choose one's attitude in any given set of circumstances, to choose one's own way." Frankl, *Man's Search For Meaning, supra,* p.86.

[3] Kanter, Rosabeth Moss. "How Great Companies Think Differently." *Harvard Business Review.* Harvard Business Publishing, 01 Nov. 2011; Collins, James C. *Good to Great: Why Some Companies Make the Leap--and Others Don't.* New York, NY: HarperBusiness, 2001. Print.

environment, then they are less susceptible to tempting offers that would cause them to compromise their values. Being upfront with constituents (partners, suppliers, distributors, customers, employees, etc.) and securing their commitment to the same values and vision at the outset of any contractual relationship will give them the ability to ground conversations about course corrections and problem solving on those key principles. No one will be surprised, and they'll have calibrated their alignment in connection with their core vision and values—what really matters—before they embark on their work together.

Integrating Discovering Agreement into the Daily Practice of Law

The first time most of my clients experience Discovering Agreement (DA) is when they receive my engagement letter. The first Touchstone statement they read is the one I have written about my own vision, mission, and values and principles for practicing law and serving clients' needs.

Creating one's own Touchstone is a very helpful learning experience. It gives one a sense of how difficult it is to form this unfamiliar type of expression. We don't usually verbalize our deepest values or most far-seeing visions. We may have "a feeling," may know when we are happy or unhappy, but we don't connect our core values or our vision of a better world with the day-to-day grind of reading and answering e-mail or holding telephone conferences. We adopt conventional practices and structures (with their embedded values and perspectives) without realizing what grafting these prefabricated belief systems onto our lives will mean. Asking oneself the questions, sweating out the verbalizations, and refining and revising a Touchstone for oneself is the first step to "being the change you want to see in the world," as Gandhi admonished.

Bringing consciousness to bear is a major game changer, as the emperor who hired that very flashy tailor can attest. For me, as a legal practitioner, DA is about bringing conscious awareness to what my own assumptions are as I prepare to assist a client with negotiating a deal, forming a contractual relationship, or dealing with the tensions that arise during performance. Applying my Touchstone to mundane, daily tasks integrates my most basic truths—transmuting vision, mission, and values and principles into living expression.

So, let's give it a try, shall we? Imagine that I am on the phone with you—I would ask and you would answer:

- If you woke up tomorrow and a miracle had happened and the core problem with our world had been solved, what would be different? What would people be doing?
- If all your problems with practicing law and with work/life integration had been solved, what would you be doing? How would you be conducting your practice, your work, your life?
- If the problems with the legal system (especially in your area of practice) had been completely solved, what would people be doing? How would legal affairs related to your area of practice be conducted?
- What is the big "Why," the "higher Yes," that you are reaching for that leads you to embrace or reject the way things are now or other ways of doing the work?
- What is it about your relationship with clients that makes it worth the time and effort to do this work?

— Write your vision statement below —
I envision a world where...

When you read your Vision statement, do you feel a rush of energy? If not, you might want to try again. As Andrew Carnegie said, "If you want to be happy, set a goal that commands your thoughts, liberates your energy, and inspires your hope." Your Vision statement should have this effect. It should inspire in you a sense of focus, energy, and hope.

Now, let's try a Mission statement.

- What are you doing now in your life and practice that serves your Vision?
- What would you like/prefer to be doing in your practice to contribute to bringing that better world into being?
- What is already happening in the legal world that is moving us all closer to the better world you envision?
- Do you want to do something to join existing efforts or keep those changes going?
- What is your current practice meant to provide in terms of "making the miracle happen" personally, professionally, and for the world?
- If you cannot see how your current practice helps make the miracle happen, then what is your current practice supposed to make happen? Why do you continue in your practice?

— Write your mission statement below —
In service of my vision, my Mission is…

Now move on to your Values & Principles:

- What are the keys to satisfaction for you to be willing to enter and continue in any client/attorney relationship?
- How do you expect (require) people (yourself and others) to behave in a working relationship?
- What sorts of behaviors are especially important to you

in the attorney/client relationship? (answer about behaviors of both attorneys and the clients)

- As an attorney, to what do you wish to habituate yourself?

Now consider your Constraints & Imperatives:

- What things will you never agree to or abide with?
- What things—actions, behaviors, and events—would cause you to terminate the attorney/client relationship?
- What things must always be true or present for you to be willing to remain in the attorney/client relationship?

— List your Values & Principles,
Constraints & Imperatives below —
**In service of my Vision and in pursuing my Mission,
I choose to practice in accordance with the following
Principles & Values...**

Using these same questions, I have developed the following Touchstone for my own practice of law:

Linda's Vision–Mission–Values Statement

Vision

I envision a world where the power of love has replaced the love of power. This vision includes a legal system that inspires and supports sustainable, beneficial, re-generative behaviors, relationships, and enterprises—a system that allows individuals, organizations, and communities to conduct all their legal affairs in alignment with their values, their principles, and their vision for a better world.

Mission

My mission is to support clients in conducting their legal affairs in alignment with their values, their principles, and their vision for a better world and to conduct myself and my practice in a way that stimulates and sustains positive effects—social, environmental, financial, and personal—for my clients, for myself and for all beings (family, friends, colleagues, our local and global communities, and future generations).

Principles & Values

In service of my vision and mission, I choose to practice in accordance with the following principles and values:

- *Winning does not require a loser*
- *Safety is mutual or it is not real safety[4]*
- *Finding ways to join forces with others and—together—designing sustainable, beneficial and enjoyable relationships and enterprises is better than approaching deal-making as an encounter between opposing forces seeking to win an advantage, one over the other*
- *Addressing conflict and crisis need not involve coercion or manipulation*
- *I expect clients to gladly take an active, fully engaged role designing and conducting each deal/ relationship/undertaking in which they engage*
- *I provide to my clients information and analysis on how*

---

[4] "Safety" as used here means having sufficient predictability, so that one's expectations are reasonably assured, enabling one to plan and venture with well-founded confidence that one will retain the power to take a meaningful role in responding to changing circumstances and will have an equal voice and be treated fairly should conflict arise.

the law and current legal system might affect their potential deal/relationship/undertaking/conflict and how to best put into words the terms and conditions of the agreements they reach with others, so that the existing system is most likely to support and protect everyone's intentions and expectations.

- *I value honesty, reliability, excellence, responsiveness, kindness, and enjoyment. I believe that integrity (consciously aligning one's actions with one's deeply held values) is the cornerstone of any worthwhile endeavor. Each person acting in integrity and taking responsibility for his or her own actions and desires is key to my enjoyment and willingness to work with anyone.*

- *I value honest communication and striving for clarity even when it is uncomfortable.*

- *When it comes to both personal and professional behavior, I believe the best guide is the Golden Rule.*

Conscious Engagement

Entering an attorney/client engagement with a DA conversation gives lawyer and client an opportunity to check in a meaningful way that their expectations for the relationship are aligned. Though there are some exceptions, most "client intake" forms gather only factual information. Crafting Touchstones at the outset helps both attorney and potential clients assess whether this is a relationship that they want to enter and also clarifies the underlying assumptions upon which decisions and plans will be based.

Assumptions both lawyers and clients carry into the relationship create an inherent logic for decision making. Unexamined assumptions can impose a logic contrary to one's vision and lead to thwarted aspiration and unnecessary conflict. Becoming aware of underlying assumptions enables us to make intentional choices about whether we align with the default, cultural assumptions or have different ideas.

Some of the assumptions that we as lawyers tend to hold about our role include: I—as lawyer—am the appropriate person to negotiate on behalf of the client as their proxy—shielding the client from the experience of engaging in the adversarial conversation; the party that I will negotiate with is going to be focused on trying to intimidate me and take advantage of my client (and they will expect the same of me); my job is to try and predict, to the greatest extent possible, everything that might go wrong with the proposed relationship and endeavor, and to get the other party to agree to bear the greater burden of risk in every instance.

These are assumptions many of us have adopted without consciously considering whether we agree with them. Our culture and its stories about the law and lawyers paint a picture that we unthinkingly adopt and then try to live by. Taking the time to directly examine and consider our underlying assumptions about what we and our clients expect of "a lawyer" opens up a freedom of choice for us about how we want to design our lives and practices.

Additionally many clients treat the call to the lawyer the way they'd order a pizza. "I need a sales and distribution agreement, heavy on the decision-making control, give me extra royalties, and super-size the territory." They dictate the deal points (usually the agreed amount of money to be paid and a description of the services or goods to be provided in exchange) and they expect the lawyer to whip a template document out of a file drawer, customize it to fit the deal points, and send it out for signature.

Often, they are not far off in their expectations. Lawyers do tend to work from "go-bys." It shortens the time needed to prepare the document, which is good for the client in terms of cost savings on the lawyer's fee. Lawyers also use their template forms to supply road-tested language for the legal "boilerplate," such as indemnification clauses, choice of law, force majeure, and other impenetrable, arcane provisions that clients ignore and lawyers obsess over, along with whatever else the lawyer believes will serve the client's interests. Clients tend to assume that the boilerplate will do what it is intended to do. They rarely read it. In my experience, most business people do not fully realize or care what the boilerplate means or why it should be in the document. They generally want one- or two-page agreements and, almost universally, are certain that the best part to cut is all that crazy boilerplate gobbledy-gook.

If you wish to take a different approach to supporting your clients in their contract formation, drafting and performance, then addressing the difference and confirming with the client that they see the value of your approach is best done in the earliest stage of the attorney/client relationship. Get clear about what their assumptions are and whether those are consistent with how you choose to practice, what you expect of your clients, and the service you are willing and able to offer.

This is why I ask potential clients to provide their Touchstone statement to include in our engagement letter. If the idea of a Touchstone is unfamiliar to them, I will generally offer an explanation of why I believe it is valuable for me to fully understand their priorities, not only in terms of the matter about which they want my help, but also what are their overall business goals and priorities. We talk about their "big why" and about what their assumptions and expectations are with regard to my role and theirs in the attorney/client relationship.

I ask questions and engage in reflective listening until they can confirm that I have understood. It is important to accept that the client may not find this sort of conversation easy. They may say that they do not have time for it. My response is to check with them—to ask if they are saying that they don't see value in my having a complete and accurate understanding of what really matters to them and their business. Sometimes it is at this point in the conversation that I realize this is not a client I will enjoy working with. Other times, this is the point at which the attorney/client relationship deepens and becomes meaningful in a way that both I and the client truly enjoy. The connection created by exploring why the client is seeking a lawyer, why the client wants to work with me and why I want to work with that client calibrates alignment of our expectations, and helps us clarify the governing principles for how we will work together.

Having asked the questions, reflected back the answers, and explored for deeper meanings, I then will ask if the client would like to draft their own Touchstone, or if they would like me to write a first draft for their review. If I am to do the first pass at drafting their Touchstone, I often will do more research—checking their website and reviewing press reports. Then, incorporating my notes from our conversation, I make my best guess as to their Vision, Mission, Values & Principles, and Constraints & Imperatives. I send the draft to them and request revisions or complete replacement (if my suggestions are not accurate or complete). No one likes to be misunderstood. It is my experience that if I have gotten something wrong, they will correct me.

If the client does not do any revisions, if they just adopt my proposed Touchstone without objections, then I take that as a red flag. I will revisit the question of accuracy and completeness in discussing the ACED provisions that are included in the engagement letter. They may have some revisions when it comes time to commit to making their Touchstone the basis for future decision making, problem solving, and dispute resolution between us in our attorney/client relationship.

Sometimes I find it is helpful to have alternative "vocabulary" to identify and characterize the Touchstone elements. Not everyone connects to "vision, mission, values" as terms that have compelling meaning. In conventional contract language, a desiccated statement of the parties' intentions and interests will sometimes appear at the beginning of the document. This often will be called "background" and is part of the WHEREAS recitations. (Whereas A wants a carpenter; and Whereas B is a carpenter who wants work...).

Where I might otherwise have used "Touchstone" as a header, I occasionally use "Background," because that word is so familiar. However, when it comes to integrating the so-called background statements into the Addressing Change and Engaging Disagreement (ACED) provisions, the word can be a little awkward. Another alternative that I have used is "Foundations." Mission can sometimes be called "Intention" or "Goals." Naming the Touchstone and its various elements should be more about the parties sharing a confirmed, mutual understanding of the meaning and value of the statements, and less about following any particular form or model.

It can also be helpful to explore with a new client the spectrum of typical approaches to conflict and discuss their tendencies when faced with tensions or dispute within business relationships. Questions to ask might include:

- What is your usual response to conflict (some people avoid it, some try to accommodate, some tend to offer compromise...)?
- "How would you like to engage conflict?"

Recognizing their default responses to conflict enhances the lawyer's ability to notice and help the client shift from an automatic reaction to a more considered and appropriate response to a given conflict situation.[5]

Other Practices

---

[5] Fred Kofman provides a good review of typical approaches to conflict in "Conscious Business" (Chapter 6: Constructive Negotiation), p. 167.

I have mentored many attorneys who are integrating DA into their practices. Each person who engages the work develops their own way of applying it based on their own client/attorney relational style. One example is attorney, Glenn Meier, who practices in Las Vegas, Nevada, and has developed his own unique approach for facilitating clients in the creation of a Touchstone. Here, in his own words, is how Glenn describes his process.

Glenn Meier:

I have found that conscious engagement with a new client, especially the development of the Cornerstone[6] can present a challenge for the practitioner for multiple reasons. At the outset, people often struggle to find language to express their feelings on subjects such as their vision for a better world or their core values. Biologically, the language center in the brain is in a different location from the part of the brain where emotions lie. Have you ever watched someone struggle to answer the question of why they love their spouse? People struggle to answer such questions because they are trying to bridge the literal gap between the emotional and the language centers of their brains.

It can be helpful to remind clients that there is immense power in operating a business with a focus on the businesses purpose, its "Why." Such a business approach attracts customers who strongly identify with the business purpose and that identification tends to foster immense loyalty among the customers.

---

[6] I use the term "Cornerstone" in my practice, rather than Touchstone, as I like for my clients (primarily business owners) to think of their "vision, mission, values" statement as the foundation for their business decisions going forward. The two terms are, for purposes of this work, functionally equivalent.

Appreciating the value in having a strong Cornerstone, encourages everyone to bring focus and attention to its development.

My legal training has proved valuable as I help clients grapple with expressing their Cornerstone statement. Lawyers are trained to be meticulously precise with language. We understand the nuances of language and are accustomed to articulating general concepts expressed by our clients into specific legal language. Lawyers who supplement their legal analytical skills with strong emotional intelligence skills can merge these talents to aid clients in articulating their business Cornerstone in a way that can easily be shared with the world. This supports the clients in operating a truly "Why" focused organization.

Another challenge I've found in helping clients develop their Cornerstone during the engagement process is the fact that, by definition, the lawyer and the client have had minimal opportunity to develop a strong connection before undertaking this task. As a result, the client may not yet be fully comfortable with sharing things that really reveal their inner self. Unless someone is particularly open they may resist engaging in a process that essentially starts with a virtual stranger asking, "tell me your life's purpose."

To alleviate these issues, I use a process that combines indirect "getting to know you" type questions with analysis of the client's language to begin developing my understanding of the Client's Cornerstone. My process involves three meetings with some homework in between for both the lawyer and the client.

Initial Meeting –

The purpose of the initial meeting is for me to interview the client. I see my job as nothing more than to ask questions. I strive not to perform any analysis of the client responses during this interview; analysis comes later. That later analysis involves looking at the client's precise language so it is my practice to record the interview. I've found that audio recording is sufficient. While a video recording of the first interview can give the opportunity to observe the client's body language, the critical analysis is focused on the client's verbal language.

The physical environment for the interview is important. The key, in my experience, is to have a setting where I and the client can be comfortable. I try to minimize physical barriers between me and the client. For example, I avoid conducting the interview while sitting behind a desk. Soft background music can help set a good tone, but I always ensure that any background sounds will not interfere with the recording.

I start by letting the client know that I will be asking some general questions, and that there are no right or wrong answers. I just want to learn more about the client's background, and encourage the client to respond with the first thoughts that come to mind. If the client seems uncomfortable, I encourage them to think of this process as a game.

I begin the interview by telling about how—as a kid—when I read comic books, my favorite issues were the ones that told "origin stories," the stories of the events that transformed the main characters from a regular person into a superhero! Origins tell the story of what propelled the hero into becoming their most extraordinary self, be it Peter Parker getting bitten by a radioactive spider and transforming into the Amazing Spiderman or Bruce Wayne witnessing his parents murder and embarking on a life of crime fighting as the Caped Crusader, Batman. I want to discover (and often to help the client discover) what has propelled them to where they are today.

With that introduction, I ask the client to tell their origin story. I try to keep the questions very general and avoid providing parameters for my client's response. My aim is to spark a conversation that the client feels free to take in whatever direction strikes a chord with them.

Once the client begins their origin story, I allow them to go at their own pace. For me, the key is to get the client saying as much as possible; I like to hear as many of the client's words as reasonably possible, and I engage in active listening, drawing out details as needed, but keeping the spotlight on the client.

If the client is a business owner I will generally also ask for the origin story of their business. Again, I try to talk as little as possible, only saying what is necessary to draw the client out.

After we've gone through the origin story, I ask the client to tell me about some thing or things that make them angry. Here I may become a bit more active in my follow up questioning, trying to draw the particulars out from the client about what specifically makes them angry asking them for examples of specific events or activities. From there I ask the client to describe an activity or activities they do where they can find themselves losing track of time, something that they devote significant time to without worrying about what comes back to them. Finally, I ask the client to name two or three favorite animals, asking what characteristics of the animals they admire. Generally this interview takes somewhere between sixty and ninety minutes.

Homework Following First Meeting –

Both I and the client have homework assignments following the initial meeting. The client's homework is relatively straightforward. I ask them to complete a values assessment and be prepared to discuss the results at the follow on meeting. The Barret Values Centre (www. barretvaluescentre.com) offers an easy to use, free online assessment and that is an excellent resource.

My homework following the first meeting is more in depth, but I find it highly valuable in developing a deeper understanding of my client. I review the recording of the conversation, listening to discern the client's feelings on certain points.[7]

I find that our feelings on various topics generally can be sorted into one of five buckets: things we have neutral feelings about; things we have positive feelings for; things we have negative feelings for; things we have strongly positive feelings for; and things we have strongly negative feelings for. Neutral topics are those that provoke little if any response. For example, relaying basic factual information is likely a neutral topic: "the store closes at six."

---

[7] I learned this analysis process through studying a word mapping technique developed by Dave Logan, author of "Tribal Leadership." For more information about the word mapping technique, see Dave's blog post at http://www.culturesync.net/learn-instant-rapport-in-18-minutes/.

Most topics will produce some level of either positive or negative response. Some will stimulate mild feelings while others will produce more intense feelings. I am listening to the client's words focusing on how it seems each subject makes the client feel. Like anything, this type of listening can be challenging at first; however, practice has helped me become more adept at identifying the feelings that underlie people's spoken words.

My goal for this process is to identify those things that generate the most intense response in the client which, in turn, helps me discern the client's core values. I pay particular attention to events described by the client that produced both a strong reaction and action on the client's part. Those tend to be the things that lie at the client's core.

There are some interview questions I've specifically chosen to elicit certain reactions. Obviously asking someone about what makes them angry will generally lead to topics that produce a strong negative reaction. Asking people to describe activities where they tend to lose track of time helps me identify activities where the person is in or near a "flow" state.[8] In that state people generally feel highly aligned with their values, so learning when the client tends to experience flow provides additional insight into the client's values.

Recall that I ask my client questions during the initial interview about an animal or animals they like. By learning about something external to the client that they admire, I find I am likely to learn more about traits the client would like to see in themselves.

---

[8] Csikszentmihalyi, Mihaly. *Flow: The Psychology of Optimal Experience.* New York: Harper & Row, 1990. Print.

The combination of the indirect questions used in the interview along with the word mapping technique provides me insight into the things that my client values in life, and I make a list of those. From there, I evaluate which of those items I think are the client's core values, those things about which I have the impression the client simply will not compromise. I note these items on my own list of "client values."

Second Meeting –

I begin the next meeting by confirming that the client has completed their values assessment. Then I tell them about my homework and ask if I may share some of my observations from that process. I try to remain aware of the underlying cultural expectation that lawyers are people in a position of authority. My intention is to keep the client in the position of authority when it comes to identifying what really matters to them. In sharing my impressions, I follow the general format of, "it seems like XYZ is something that is important to you" and just follow the discussion as it goes.

The client can share their own self insight, amplified by their experience with the values assessment tool. Together the client and I extract a list of values and a sense of how the client prioritizes those values. The goal of this undertaking is to develop a written expression of the client's list of core values.

Starting with the client's values, as opposed to the client's vision or sense of their mission may seem a little backwards. After all, we have our values as tools to help us fulfill our vision and our mission. While it is true that our values must exist under the umbrella of these other items, I find that people's values are relatively more concrete and this typically makes it easier for them to discuss values.

Additionally, my effort to discern the client's values helps to develop a strong connection between me and client. Even if it turns out that my insights into the client's values are inaccurate, the simple fact that I have made a concerted effort to truly understand the client can help establish a relatively deep connection between myself and the client in a short time. We each have a richer, more robust understanding of one another as people, what it is like to work together, and how we would like to orient decisions and problem solving.

With the client's values in hand, the balance of this meeting is aimed at encouraging the client to reflect on their vision and mission. My purpose at this point is not to develop a formal statement of these items, but rather to encourage general thinking on these subjects. To get the client thinking about vision, I enquire what they see when they think about the world being a better place. To help them as they articulate their mission, I ask for insights on how the client's talents might be used to help bring about this vision.

Clients sometimes get stuck in these areas—the point where the gap in the brain's geography between feeling and thinking is at its widest—and may need help finding the right language to express themselves. I try to remain alert and careful that I am trying to simply extract the client's thoughts rather than supply my own language for what I think the client's vision and mission should be.

Once this second meeting is complete, the client will have a solid sense of how to think about and articulate their values, including which of their values are core values. The meeting also will have stimulated their thinking about vision and mission and they are prepared to put together a draft of their Cornerstone statement.

Homework Following Second Meeting –

The client now has the task of developing an expression of their Cornerstone. I encourage the client to begin the Cornerstone statement by setting forth their Vision; their expression of what a better world looks like. Following the Vision, comes a statement of the client's mission, how they see their actions leading to the better world they envision. Finally, there is the client's list of values as previously developed. As part of that list, I ask the client to include a list of needs and constraints. Needs are things that must be present in order for the client to feel aligned (must haves), and constraints are factors that cannot be present (can't haves). These items reflect the client's core values. The core values are the things on which the client will not compromise.

I encourage clients to find their own "voice" in writing out their Cornerstone. No particular type of language is necessary. It is far more important for the client to use language that "sounds like them" than it is to find a specific format or style for the language. I remind them that the Cornerstone is a tool that they will use over and over in guiding their decisions. It should be a tool that fits them comfortably.

My homework following the second meeting is to outline what I anticipate will go into a client's Cornerstone. I specifically do not write out my prediction for the client's Cornerstone, but rather just put together a bulleted list of items I anticipate seeing in their Cornerstone. I believe writing out a full version of the client's Cornerstone runs the risk of substituting my voice for the client. I use my list during the follow on meeting as a cross check for items to review with the client.

Third Meeting –

The purpose of the final meeting in this process is to actually finalize the client's Cornerstone. I begin by asking the client to review their Cornerstone with me. One thing I watch for particularly is any items that surprise me. Given the preparatory work that has gone into the process to this point, there should be nothing that surprises me, so if a surprise comes up it will warrant further discussion with the client. The other thing I am paying the most attention to is whether any elements that I anticipated being part of a client's Cornerstone are missing. If so, I raise those items with the client.

It is important to note that I am not looking to edit the client or to catch a "mistake" on their part. It's merely to act as a reflector for the client to make sure they have covered everything they want to in the Cornerstone. Once we have reviewed the Cornerstone in its entirety, I run the client through a few scenarios that demonstrate how the Cornerstone might be used. For my clientele of business owners I present hypothetical business decisions with multiple potential responses and talk through with the client how those potential responses appear through the lens of the Cornerstone.

How the client responds to these scenarios is not important so long as the client can confidently state that their chosen response is aligned with their

Cornerstone. My purpose in running through these scenarios is simply to get the client used to incorporating their Cornerstone into the decision making process.

Once the client's Cornerstone is set we can use it as a guide during future consultations. I suggest to clients that they review their Cornerstone annually to ensure that the words still fit for them. Overtime, someone's vision may evolve or they may undertake a new mission to help them realize that vision. Periodic reviews of the Cornerstone helps people make sure they have a vital tool to help them maintain constant integrity between their actions and their ideals.

CHAPTER 8

Playing Well with Others

Even if the other party to a client's contract clings to the conventional playbook, the Discovering Agreement (DA) oriented lawyer and client can operate from a position of integrity, which gives them a strength that arises from being able to see and assess opportunities, choices, and possibilities without falling victim to the old emotional triggers that can draw us into a destructive spiral. The job, when trying to interrupt the destructive pattern, is to shift focus and choose a different logic tree, presenting the other party with an array of choices that may not follow the conventional script. By refusing to follow the pattern, we change the pattern.

Most people assume that for DA to be useful, both parties have to sign on to a "new way" of engaging the negotiation and drafting process, but DA is a transparent application. Because it makes intuitive sense to nonlawyers, it can be surprisingly easy to introduce and implement.

Just Do It

There is no need to say "We do things differently"—just do them differently. I have never found a need to try and introduce DA concepts or elements. I never say "I have a new way of negotiating and drafting contracts that I'd like you to try."

Typically, I work with my client—the person who is the

human (often nonlawyer) representative of my client, the person who will be living the deal—and together we prepare a Touchstone statement specific to the contemplated contractual relationship. As has been discussed, this improves clarity, supports the client in determining their "BATNA,"[1] and provides a backstop against reactiveness. It also serves to set a new pattern. I ask the client to also imagine what the Touchstone for the other party might be, and we prepare a statement that we believe reflects the other party's core interests, boundaries, principles, and goals. Then, as early as possible in the negotiation conversation, my client e-mails both Touchstones to the person who will be their coparty, their counterpart in living the deal—human to human.

This message can be as informal or formal as is appropriate to the situation and the parties' relationship. I find it is good to include three things: (i) the client's Touchstone; (ii) our best guess at the other party's Touchstone; and (iii) the queries: Have we been accurate? Did we miss anything?

The e-mail might use language along the following lines:

I find that the most rewarding and smoothest running business relationships are based on a foundation that is more than decisions about particular deal points. I would like to confirm that we are on the same page about the things that are going to matter most to each of us as the work progresses. In other words, I'd like to get familiar with our respective bottom-lines (beyond the financial imperatives). What I'm interested in are the priorities that will be the main decision-drivers for each of us.

Here is our vision for the relationship/transaction/endeavor [...]; and these are the principles and values that are key to everything we do [...]. These are the boundaries that we consider essential in working together and in conducting our business and our lives [...]; and these are our goals for the relationship/transaction/endeavor [...]. This is why we are

---

[1] Best Alternative to a Negotiated Agreement.

choosing to work with you [...].

Because we believe this sort of transparency and understanding is key to forming a worthwhile and successful agreement, we would like to know what are your guiding vision and principles, important boundaries, goals for the transaction/relationship/endeavor, and why you are choosing to work with us. We've made a guess, based on our experience with your organization and based on information your organization provides online. Would you let us know if we're on the right track? Or if there is something we've missed or not correctly understood about what really matters for your organization in this proposed relationship/transaction/endeavor?

As the client moves forward into the conversation with their co-party, I facilitate reflective listening, assisting both the client and the other party in exploring and articulating accurate and complete Touchstone statements.

The other party may not respond to the Touchstone request at all. When this happens, I don't let it worry me. The client has put out there what matters to them, and what they believe matters to their coparty. They've changed the conversation, and introduced a new option for interaction.

If the other party does come back with a response, they may say, "Perfect. Yep. Love it. We are all on the same page." And they may be—or they may be just saying what they think will move the deal forward and get them to whatever their goal is. We will have the opportunity to check this when we send them our proposed contract or a red line of their proposed contract.

Getting the Touchstone "right" (accurate and complete for each party to that party's satisfaction) becomes a more compelling interest when the parties recognize that their Touchstone forms the foundation and focus for their conversations about how best to respond in the face of change or disagreements during their shared endeavor. When a party blithely agrees to sign a Statement of Agreement without truly participating in the conversation about the content and meaning of the foundational Touchstone/s, it is important to give serious thought to what this might indicate about the mindset of that party, and what may remain unexamined.

—Example: "I'll sign anything you want."

"Jane" was eager to join the team. She had lots of ideas and energy. The team was looking forward to having the extra set of hands and anticipated a lightened load with a new, congenial colleague. The team sent Jane a draft Statement of Agreement and asked her to amend the Touchstone if what they had drafted was not accurate or complete. She simply signed the document and sent it back saying that she would sign anything they asked, she just wanted to be as supportive as she could be. Trusting that Jane had carefully read the Touchstone and was fully aligned with its meaning, the team welcomed Jane on board.

As their work together moved forward, the team began to notice that Jane was often not willing to accept tasks they asked her to do, but was setting out on her own initiative and undertaking tasks without team preapproval or what the team considered to be necessary supervision. When the team tried to address what they saw as an overstepping of roles and responsibilities, Jane grew silent and sulky. It was becoming evident that Jane held a perspective and set of expectations that were not in line with the team's. Her expectation was that she would have full autonomy in choosing and carrying out her responsibilities, along with broad access to the business' confidential information. The team had intended that Jane's autonomy and access would be increased on a slow, gradual basis after a period of careful supervision, and not until they felt certain that the team and Jane were fully in sync.

The crisis came when the team leader phoned Jane to discuss an e-mail Jane had sent out that the team leader felt was not completely appropriate for Jane's role. Jane immediately became highly emotional, angrily issuing an ultimatum that either the team give her the autonomy she wanted or she would quit.

When Jane's unrecognized expectations were thwarted, a strong emotional reaction was triggered. The team was astonished by the suddenness and strength of Jane's fury. Sadly, Jane's anger and frustration left her unwilling to engage in a collaborative conversation. She instead chose to hold firm to her ultimatum. The team would have to agree to her terms or she would leave.

The Addressing Change and Engaging Disagreement (ACED) provisions merely said, "If we find ourselves in disagreement, we agree to talk together in good faith to find a way of moving forward that works for everyone and is in alignment with our stated Vision, Mission, and Values." But unstructured conversations were too fraught with emotion and rapidly devolved into personal attacks from Jane and confusion and anger from the team leader. Because the ACED section of their contract did not have specific steps for initiating a restorative conflict conversation, the team found that they could not engage Jane in meaningful dialogue about the problems. She and the team parted ways.

Both Jane and the team leader would have benefitted from a structure that gave them time and space to gather their thoughts and open a conversation with a reminder of the beneficial purposes they had come together to achieve, and they needed a framework sturdy enough to allow Jane to express her strong emotions without trapping herself in an ultimatum.

Had Jane been willing and able to engage in a meaningful dialogue, the work of recognizing and expressing a true foundational Touchstone for everyone would have become the necessary first step in that conversation. Because they did not have a true and complete expression of expectations at the outset, the parties' relationship was unstable. Their expectations were in conflict. Had this been realized in the formation stage of the relationship, before anyone's expectations were actually disappointed, it would have been possible for the parties to either adjust everyone's expectations to more closely match reality, or they could have decided that the relationship was not one they wanted to enter. The sudden eruption of this acrimonious and destructive conflict might have been avoided and the benefits Jane and the team hoped for would have had a better chance of coming to fruition.

When both parties do not take full self-responsibility for the Touchstone and Commitment to the ACED process, conflict is more likely to arise and escalate rapidly because the coparties do not have the clarity and buy-in required for true alignment. Conducting the conflict will likely be more difficult and involve doing the very work that was left undone at the outset, the work of exploring, expressing, and calibrating the vision, mission, values, constraints, and imperatives (expectations and requirements) of all parties.

If a coparty appears not to meaningfully participate in the drafting or does not take co-ownership of the Touchstone statement, it is worthwhile to bring attention to the fact. I let the parties know that I am not certain they really have an authentic and robust foundational understanding of one another's expectations. I encourage them to really do the thinking about their own keys to satisfaction, about what they would consider incompatible actions, etc. I remind them that while contracts typically limit the description of "expectations and requirements" to production milestones, payment terms, quality control provisions, etc. (the "deal points"), experience teaches that there are other important expectations and requirements in play such as relational behavior; cultural imprints; and unspoken assumptions about authority, autonomy, and communication.

Buy-in

Getting buy-in to this clarification process at the outset will increase the stability and resiliency of the parties' relationship. One way to do this is to ask the parties if they can see the benefit of getting clear about these things at this early stage, and what downside they can imagine might result if they aren't clear. Having the parties actually verbalize the upside of genuine participation and the downside of failing to do so, helps secure and affirm their buy-in to both the foundational mindset and the DA process.

If I find they are unwilling to engage in a genuine exploration of the meaning behind what they are setting out to do together, then I remind my client that they will be relying on whatever dispute resolution system is adopted (either by default or by contractual provision) for dealing with conflicts that might otherwise have been avoided or made less disruptive. I also strongly encourage the parties to include a contractual provision making participation in a preexisting collaborative conflict resolution process (such as joint-session mediation or interest-based mediation) a precondition to the use of any other dispute resolution process. I find that designating a particular collaborative structure for addressing issues that arise between them (even without a Touchstone statement or other structured dialogue provision), somewhat reduces the chances of intractable conflict and destruction of the benefits the relationship was formed to achieve.

Introducing ACED Provisions

My practice is to include proposed ACED provisions when I send a "redlined" revised contract over to the other party (or their attorney). I include a comment that says something like, "Here's what we suggest as a way to avert unnecessary conflict and use moments of disagreement as ways to improve things for everyone involved. These are suggested procedures that have a proven track record of success. Our intention is to put in place a way to solve problems quickly with the least expense in terms of time, money, and the parties' working relationship." This is always enough to open a conversation about why this alternative approach is being requested. Both my client and I stand ready to engage in a conversation about what we don't like about the way the current, conventional system impacts parties when they are trying to solve problems.

The client can tell her/his counterpart that the provisions are suggested because they would like to give everyone a way to talk about it if one or both parties begin to feel dissatisfied or uncomfortable about how things are going. Most people would much rather have a way to bring up difficult topics and get them productively resolved than let them become an awkwardness and eventual obstacle to getting to the goals and achieving the potential that they share by joining forces successfully.

No proposed conversational structure or system is ever etched in stone. It is a suggestion, a starting place for the parties to explore together what they would like to put in place to serve the purpose of "enforcing promises and holding each other accountable" without the expense and destructiveness of conventional adversarial approaches, and maybe even with a productive, creative result coming from any conflict. The discussion can be started with questions, such as "What do you usually do when you become dissatisfied with how a contractual relationship is going? How has this approach worked for you in the past, did it work well? Have you had bad experiences in the past—where things went south when you thought they needn't have? What would you do differently, in hindsight?

Integrating Touchstone and ACED into the Contract Document

Parties often put the Touchstone at the beginning of the contract, as a Preamble or as part of the Recitations. Others prefer to use it in place of an arbitration clause. Another option is to create an Exhibit that holds the Touchstone and ACED provisions and is incorporated into the contract by reference.

Many clauses and provisions in a DA Statement of Agreement remain the same as they would appear in a conventional contract document. Plain English is a characteristic that many practitioners of "Conscious Contracts"[2] believe is key. For me, plain English is not a goal, but a result of a DA mindset. The use of Touchstone and ACED provisions obviates the need for much of the dense and murky legalese we have become inured to in the practice of law. The murkiness is often the result of efforts to eliminate ambiguity. The DA approach acknowledges the inevitability of ambiguity and provides a way to engage it without devolving into a battle of interpretation. The Touchstone and ACED frame and framework enable the parties to explore the possibilities and implications of ambiguity, complexity, and context. It is a conversation of the parties, by the parties, and for the parties in their unique situation, with their particular needs, interests, vision, and mission. Another happy consequence is that DA Statements of Agreement tend to be shorter documents as there is less that needs to be predicted and controlled.

No Enemies

Many conventional approaches to negotiation include a set of stratagems that have been developed in order to manipulate the other party. For instance, some negotiation gurus advise that we try to discourage deceptiveness in the other party by—among other things—implying that we have a strong alternative to accepting an offer from the other party, suggesting the other party has limited options to doing the deal with us, or reminding the other party of the legal implications of unethical behavior. It appears that the underlying premise of these tactics is the belief that the other party is an adversary—an enemy. Seeing the other party as an adversary puts the relationship into combat mode where fight/flight, attack/defend/counterattack, and

---

[2] Wright, J. Kim. "Conscious Contracts: Bringing Purpose and Values into Legal Documents." Web log post. *Jkimwright.com,* 30 July 2015. Web. 28 July 2015; "Conscious Contracts." Conscious Contracts.com Web. 28 Aug. 2015.

manipulate/obfuscate are logical options.

The radical truth I have learned is that one can be effective without holding this premise. I am not alone in this. The lives and work of many, much more visible people throughout history have shown that dropping enemy images is core to a creative, expansive, nonviolent response to differences and conflict. Most familiar among them are Gandhi, Dr. Martin Luther King, Jr., and Nelson Mandela. These heroic lives answer the next question that is so often raised: "What if there is unequal bargaining power?" and "What if the other party clings to the 'enemy images' mode?" Either of these situations might make the emotional journey more challenging; but, as history demonstrates, neither means that one has to adopt an adversarial model in order to take powerful and effective action. Holding to principles is far more helpful in Discovering Agreement than is a bag of negotiating tricks. Holding to core values and knowing our guiding vision and mission make us less susceptible to these tricks and provo-cations and does away with our need to resort to trickery ourselves.

Other negotiating tactics offered are about building rapport between the parties—highlight things you have in common (shared social networks, similar age, job history, life experience, common or linked goals, etc.). These efforts may seem similar to the DA approach, but are often disingenuous and may be entered into with the intent to manipulate the other party into accepting terms they might otherwise reject. By opening the conversation in terms of exploring and sharing Vision, Mission, Values, Constraints, Imperatives, Core Principles & Values, Keys to Satisfaction and the like, the DA process begins with authentic, mutual comprehension of whether the parties are indeed aligned, rather than manufacturing a rapport in order to paper over an adversarial attitude.

From a Discovering Agreement perspective, there is no such thing as an enemy. There's Me, knowing what really matters, what's okay and what's not, there's You, telling me what really matters, what's okay and what's not, and based on the calibration of our respective Touchstones, we have discovered whether we are able and willing to form an Us.

What if someone is lying about their Vision, Mission, Values statement (VMV) in order to get us into the deal? How do we know they'll abide by the VMV? This is where the condition precedent component of the ACED provision comes into play. When the parties face the question of whether they will commit to making the Touchstone-centric ACED conversation a precondition to litigation or any other adversarial proceeding, we discover whether the parties are truly willing to put their money where their mouth is.

If something goes wrong, if someone is not living up to their obligations, will both parties be comfortable using the Touchstone as their guidance system and frame for the courageous conversation that will need to take place? Or do they find that one or both would rather be able to go directly to an adversarial arena where they can argue their viewpoint and seek coercion? If the Touchstone they have stated is not true or if it is incomplete, the parties are less likely to be willing to make it the foundation for measuring the appropriateness of future decisions and resolutions.

Responding to Common Objections

It is not unusual for a party or counsel who is unfamiliar with nonadversarial approaches to object to the inclusion of Touchstone and ACED provisions. I see this as an opportunity to ask about what the underlying concern is that causes the other person to object. Sometimes objections are based in fears that a commitment to nonadversarial conflict will leave the party vulnerable. Nonadversarial approaches are often characterized as weak or soft. If possible, I talk this through with my client or with the other party and their counsel. In my experience, trying to convince or persuade them to see things from my point of view is not an effective approach. It is much more helpful to be genuinely curious about what is at the root of their concern. Some questions I ask are, "What have you found works and what doesn't work about the conventional system? What do you want your contract document to do for you? In your experience, what approaches have been effective and efficient for solving problems and getting things on the right track? What do you think would be good to know about how the other party is to work with?"

In addition to concerns about the overall safety of nonadversarial processes, it is my experience that other parties raise objections to incorporating the Touchstone and ACED provisions for one of two reasons, they worry that (i) it makes the contract too hard to interpret; or (ii) it is "not enforceable."

1. Interpretation

Interpretation can become an issue only if a third-party adjudicator is involved; but the structure of a DA contract is such that there is never a call for this. The Touchstone will only ever need to be interpreted by the parties themselves, the ones who have written those declarations and who have agreed to make them the lodestar for shared decision making/problem solving. The only time anyone needs to interpret the meaning of the Touchstone is when the parties themselves are engaging in their structured dialogue—designed specifically to help them determine meaning for themselves. If the parties are unable to reach agreement via their ACED restorative process, then they can move to adversarial proceedings and the Touchstone is no longer an issue. At most, it would play the role of "legislative intent"—potentially providing a useful reference point if there is some otherwise impregnable ambiguity to be addressed, but not coming into play if the other terms of the contract are clear. Litigation, with its third-party-decider structure, remains available, and the difficulties of interpreting terms and conditions (in accordance with and in service of precedent and The System) also remain unchanged. All that is different is that the parties have given themselves a chance at self-determination, the chance to come together, remind themselves of what really matters and, based on their core values, decide together what makes sense for them in their unique situation.

2. Enforceability

Again, with this objection, the other party is looking at the DA document as if it is going to be interpreted and enforced by a third-party adjudicator. It is not difficult to talk through what sort of language the parties need to assure themselves that the legal system, if called upon, will enforce their commitment to the Touchstone–ACED restorative response if they find themselves in conflict. We know that the courts will enforce arbitration clauses. We know that the courts will enforce the agreements reached in mediation—so long as the parties are careful to include in their agreement document language that enables the courts to do so.

3. The Third Rail

The third objection that has arisen, in my experience, is when one party absolutely refuses to commit to using the Touchstone as the guide and criteria for dispute resolution. When we've explored and dealt with the "interpretation" and "enforceability" questions, what remains is the question, "Why do you not want to commit to this?" The conversations that I have had with other parties and their counsel has led me to conclude that the reason someone will not commit to using the Touchstone as the frame for their conflict conversations is that the Touchstone is not accurate or is not complete. It is in some way insufficient to express the truth of what really matters to that party. I always invite the objecting party to revise their Touchstone, to add or remove from it whatever is needed to make it true and meaningful for them.

This is the point when a party who has just been going along and saying that they share the other's values, vision, etc. finds themselves with no place to hide. They either are actually going to adopt the principles and values stated as the foundation for the contractual relationship—or they are not. If they do not like the Touchstone as written, they can change it. If they do not want to revise the Touchstone and continue to refuse to ascribe to any Touchstone as the guiding principles for their coendeavor, my client and I have some very important information and a profound decision to make. Does the client wish go forward with this party knowing that they are unwilling to contractually commit to walking their talk? Isn't that a great thing to know at the outset?

Dealing with the Form Carved in Stone

Oftentimes, one party will send a "standard form" to the other. How often have you received a form contract that contains nonsensical terms, clauses containing sentences without subjects or objects, broken fossils of ancient cut-and-paste jobs that no one noticed were incomplete? And how often have you seen a form that has provisions that are complete nonsequiturs with no logical reason for being included? I once reviewed a contract from a Mega-Multi-National Corp that wanted my client to come to their offices and give a series of inspirational talks. Their standard form was eight long-form pages of 10-point font that included provisions requiring my client to take full responsibility for any adverse environmental impact his live, spoken presentation might have on the site where the Corp. wanted him to speak!

There are many times when clients are faced with form contracts promulgated by the other side. This tends to happen when the client is an individual or smaller company contemplating a relationship with a large corporation. Behemoths have a need for streamlined processes, and this usually means that their legal department has approved a particular form agreement. They give the form to the nonlawyer personnel who are negotiating particular types of deals with the instruction that only certain provisions are negotiable. The prospect of making changes—such as adding Touchstone and ACED provisions—causes the corporation's nonlawyer representatives much consternation. Most people in a corporation who are not in the legal department try assiduously to avoid "going to legal" for anything more than a quick review and approval based on assurances that the designated form has been used without alteration.

In such instances, I have had occasional success creating an Exhibit to the contract that contains Touchstone statements or ACED provisions (or both) that is "incorporated and made part of the contract by this reference thereto." In those instances, I find the Exhibit usually needs some sort of opening paragraph that explains why it exists. For example,

> The following statements express the parties' core, underlying interests in connection with this shared endeavor. They represent the vision(s) we hold that motivate us to persevere in our work, the mission(s) we are joining forces to accomplish, the constraints and imperatives that inform our decision making, and the values with which we want to align all our actions.
>
> The statements are meant to serve as reference points to orient and focus our conversations in support of creative, productive, and collaborative problem-

solving should we find ourselves in disagreement in the course of our relationship and work together.

If there is absolute refusal on the part of the form's owner to include DA provisions, then the client must choose whether to move forward with a conventional contract document. This does not mean that the conversation about Touchstone and conflict resolution has been wasted. To the contrary, just having the conversation about vision, mission, values, constraints, and imperatives shifts the way in which the parties relate to one another. Questions of alignment that would never have been explored have been asked and answered. The client has a better sense of what is actually going on with the other party. We both know whether the other party is open to the type of conversation the client values or whether they are going to stick to the default, adversarial posture. The client can make the choice of whether to enter the contract and relationship knowing this.

All along the way, the conventional practices and mindset are always available, but we have the option to try to shift the conversation, to set a new logic and pattern for engaging in relationship and handling conflict. The client is no worse off than they would have been had the negotiations been conducted in a solidly conventional manner, and is probably better off for having engaged their coparty in a DA conversation. The valuable bit that is missing, however, is the commitment to, and structure for, resiliency should one or the other party become dissatisfied at some point down the road.

Happily, there are many, many instances where the other party is delighted and enthusiastic about Touchstone and ACED provisions. Business people often can't believe anything this sensible and workable is even offered by a lawyer, and almost all are delighted by it. In my experience, the ones who have objected are the ones who believe that bullying and coercion are good methods for getting their way, and your client will want to know that about a party they are considering working with.

Manipulation and Lying—Illumination of Integrity

When the Discovering Agreement process is used, the levels of integrity for all parties are illuminated. Clarity is a by-product of the process, and some parties discover that their potential contracting partner is not interested in clarity. Some even find that they are afraid of clarity themselves. We sometimes imagine or unthinkingly believe that clarity equals vulnerability, that if we are open and truthful about what is important to us and what concerns us, then the relationship we are hoping to create will not come into being, or it will develop to our disadvantage.

It is an illusion to think that by not addressing concerns and fears, or by not being open about expectations and aspirations, we will magically obtain the relationship and deal we wish for. The way to get what we want is to cocreate it by design. What designer would think it a good idea to keep the purpose of the desired object a secret from the design team? Much better to connect with and get to know the one(s) we will be in relationship with and to discover whether the relationship can be all that we imagine and maybe more. We are not entering relationships because we expect them to go south. We are entering them because we believe we will benefit from joining forces. If we hide from truth and clarity, we undercut or subvert our chances of maximizing the benefit for ourselves and the other.

Some parties seek to manipulate and control the relationship, because they think that is the way to be safe and to preserve their share of the benefits that are generated by the mutual/combined effort. They believe that keeping the provisions of the contract opaque and confusing will work in their favor because that is how they build in "flexibility" (lawyers can later argue about the meaning behind the terms of the agreement in order to try and get their client's way). My friend, J. Kim Wright, tells me she once had a lawyer say to her that he believed it was his job to write confusing provisions for just this reason. In a sense, both strategies are meant to accomplish the same goal. The interest everyone is trying to serve is flexibility. Each is looking for the best way to address change and have room to adapt performance to deal with new realities, but legal haggling over contract interpretation is an expensive way to meet that need. Discovering Agreement is one alternative approach to building adaptability into the relationship and supporting vital flexibility via the wording of the document.

CHAPTER 9

Reflections

Conventional priorities and imperatives are the foundations on which our existing business and legal systems are constructed. These systemic structures, like ruts in a dirt road, tend to draw us along the same paths and patterns, dictating the logic that directs our decision making and problem solving. Because our conventional conflict paradigm is confrontational, combative, and coercive, we expect that conflict will inevitably be unpleasant and destructive—so many of us try to avoid conflict.

The idea that there is a way to engage conflict productively—without the combativeness—is surprising. It hardly seems likely. We assume that conflict must mean we have irreconcilable differences, and someone must win at the expense of the loser. Blame-throwing and responsibility shifting are our knee-jerk reactions when someone expresses dissatisfaction.

This reluctance to engage conflict often plays out as one party or the other trying to hide a problem when it first appears, or trying to fix it without alerting the other and risking a blowup. This is the well-paved road to perdition that we all know so well. Good intentions prevent the parties from seeing that things are going off the rails until the problem becomes so big or so acute that it can no longer be denied. And there the parties are—in the hell of battle, blame, accusation, demand, and counterattack.

However, there are models in existence, with robust track records of success, demonstrating that conflict can be engaged as a shared creative undertaking rather than a battle for dominance.

Most of these models are found in the Alternative Dispute Resolution arena—certain forms of "joint-session" mediation and "restorative" practices, among others.

These models, instead of looking backwards to establish blame and determine punishment, anchor the conversation in the present moment—what is the current state of affairs, what does it mean for each party, and what are the core interests for each party going forward. The past is referenced to gain understanding of the interests that motivated the actions, so that those interests can be taken into account in the current conversation and the forward-looking plan—bringing them to the surface rather than leaving them in the subterrain of the relationship where they can fester and create renewed conflict in the future.

The hallmark of these "restorative" "collaborative" processes is an emphasis from the outset on bringing into the open the deeply held values and core interests of the parties, then working together in a facilitated conversation to find ways that everyone's values and interests can be served. These processes emphasize mutual comprehension between the parties—not only the chance to speak but also the careful confirmation that what one says has been correctly understood by the other party. Self-responsibility of each party is also key in these processes. Each party must speak up about their true interests and values, must actively engage in the creation of the resolution, and actively participate in designing the plan for going forward.

The court system was intended to serve the function of resolving disputes, but it cannot handle the complexity of real life on a case-by-case basis. What if each dispute came with its own ready-made mechanism for encompassing and engaging the full complexity and context of the situation for those particular parties in that particular place and time? What if there was a viable alternative that the parties could agree to and manage for themselves, that could interface with and even (dare we hope) harness the larger existing system? Providing this is the goal of a

Discovering Agreement (DA) contract.

Contract law protects the autonomy of the parties to create their own set of rules—their own "governing law" for their relationship. So long as the terms of the contract do not conflict with the larger system of laws and public policy, The Law will uphold and the courts will enforce the terms and conditions by which the parties choose to conduct their relationship.

So let's design our ideal relationship. Let's set up the systems we want. Let's base them on the premises that we have considered and agreed should form the foundation of our undertaking and from which the logic of our decisions will grow. Taking a page from Gandhi—let's practice satyagraha—let us hold tight to truth. Not abstract, ineffable Truth, but our own, respective truths about what really matters, why we are doing the deal, why we are doing it with this deal partner, what are the keys to satisfaction for each of us in conducting an ongoing relationship, and what are the keys for each of us to making this shared effort worthwhile. Let's set up our own, preferred, proprietary system for sensing and responding to problems as they arise—one that helps us bring the relationship and endeavor back on track quickly because we've already clarified what we mean by "on track" and we have an agreed structure for conducting the crucial (sometimes difficult) conversations that must take place for true resolution to occur.

The beauty of DA is that the resolution conversation is held by and between the parties. The ones uniquely suited to comprehensive understanding of the conflict and context in all its complexity are the ones who will determine the best resolution for themselves. It is the ultimate "ad hoc" answer, a conversational structure that can accommodate shifts in context which can trigger shifts in values/priorities.

Conscious Business, Conscious Capitalism, and Conscious Contracts

Fred Kofman provides a useful definition of "conscious" as "the capacity to be aware and to choose,"[1] and this is certainly applicable and meaningful in the context of the shift from conventional practices and assumptions and mindset. But there is a further meaning embedded in the awareness and choices of those who adopt the word "conscious" for themselves and their efforts. Conscious approaches are acknowledging that mysterious reality, "consciousness." As Dr. Michael Nagler noted in his commentary on Eknath Easwaran's translation of the Upanishads, "[W]e are not that fragile body, but that which causes it to move, breathe, and be alive: consciousness…And the same consciousness is the life of all; thus, we have the explanation for both the sanctity and unity of life."[2] When someone applies or incorporates the word "conscious" into their self-identity (socially conscious entrepreneur, conscious capitalism, etc.), their self-description includes an acknowledgment of the sanctity and unity of all life and a dedication to serving and honoring that sanctity and unity.

In the rough and tumble secularity of the business world, dominated by the numbers that assess its value and the mythologies of scarcity and separateness, which underpin its patterns and logic, the practice of consciousness—holding to the truth of the sanctity and unity of all life— can be a fierce challenge. This demands a shift in focus of attention and energy, not so much to change as to expand the meaning of "success" and "wealth." Bringing the transformation the "conscious" movement wants to see in the world—business conducted as a vehicle for serving and honoring of the sanctity and unity of all

---

[1] Kofman, Fred. *Conscious Business*. Rec. 1 Sept. 2006. Sounds True, 2006. CD.

[2] Eknath, Easwaran, and Michael N. Nagler. "The Unity of Life." *The Upanishads*. Tomales, CA: Nilgiri, 2007. 265–67. Print.

life—requires a practice of satyagraha.

The conventional business belief system has its markers and measures to bolster practitioners and believers in the zero-sum, win-lose, kill-or-be-killed worldview. Emerging conscious-business Satyagrahis need their own markers and measures to help them counteract the magnetic pull of habitual thought patterns, conditioned reactions, and inherited systemic structures. Many embed these as corporate Vision and Mission statements. Some are adopting new organizational operating and governance systems[3] along with intentionally designing and supporting cultures of compassion and empathy within their workplaces.[4] However, at the interface of business and law—the point where the business entity must engage through the vehicle of contracts to bring structure and safety to business relationships using the mechanisms of the conventional legal system—these markers and measures of consciousness seem to fade into obscurity. With a profound sense of unease, the Conscious-Business person approaching contract formation finds themselves in what appears to be an inevitably adversarial arena designed to handle conflict based on a foundational belief that conflict necessarily requires combat, a struggle to overcome opposition and gain control over outcomes.

DA enables a Conscious Business to use contract negotiation and the contract document to embed markers, measures, and systemic structures that create coherence, that will counteract conditioned responses to tensions, disagreements, and disruptive change by evoking a conscious response (the capacity to be

---

[3] Examples include, Holacracy, BCorp, and Benefit Corporations.
[4] "Why Fostering a Culture of Compassion in the Workplace Matters -K@W." *KnowledgeWharton Why Fostering a Culture of Companionate Love in the Workplace Matters Comments.* Wharton School of the University of Pennsylvania, 2 Apr. 2014. Web. 28 Aug. 2015; Morin, Amy. "Introducing A Little Compassion to Your Workplace Culture Has Big Benefits." *Forbes.* Forbes Magazine, 24 June 2015. Web. 28 Aug. 2015; Fryer, Bronwyn. "The Rise of Compassionate Management (Finally)." *Harvard Business Review.* Harvard Business Publishing, 18 Sept. 2013. Web. 28 Aug. 2015.

aware and to choose)—triggering awareness and intentional choice in circumstances that otherwise invite and encourage reversion to the world view of scarcity, separateness, and the efficacy of coercion.

Collaborative Power starts from a frame of interdependence. Winning does not require a loser. Safety must be mutual or it is not true safety. The benefits of joining forces will be far greater than the benefits of opposing forces or going it alone. The Discovering Agreement logic calls the parties to honor equally one another's core interests and deeply held values, key motivations, expectations, boundaries, and requirements, and to justify every decision on the basis that it serves everyone's needs. Discovering Agreement creates synergy.

If both parties are committed to a "conscious" approach, if they both acknowledge and commit to the reality that their well-being is interdependent (with one another and with all the stakeholders), then the lawyer's role is to watch for any place where the conventional system applies back-pressure, where our habitual attitudes and practices arise from, trigger, and perpetuate adversarial logic.

If only one party is committed to a conscious approach and working from the "reality of interdependence" mindset, then the same watchfulness holds true—and might need to be magnified. When one's coparty is operating from an adversarial or scorekeeping mindset and speaking the language of dominance and coercion, the task of remaining true to one's values and not falling into the habitual logic loop is that much more challenging.

What Discovering Agreement Is Not

Don't imagine that the DA Touchstone and Addressing Change and Engaging Disagreement (ACED) provisions are all that is needed, and don't imagine Discovering Agreement will be a pain-free, smooth, easy process. It might be, but more often we humans do things the painful, messy way. What DA does is provide a framework that encourages and redirects attention towards pain-reducing, clarity-developing, positive-spiral logic, and choice making. It is a container for the parties' best intentions, and an early alert system for calling on their "better angels." However, the ultimate responsibility for what sort of attention and mindset, for the choices that are made, for fine-tuning and implementing their agreements, rests with the parties themselves.

The leap is that the parties are taking responsibility for designing and conducting their relationship, engaging conflicts and creating benefits, rather than off-loading onto "hired-gun" or expert attorneys/representatives. Lawyers serve as counselors who help the parties navigate the interface with the larger, legal system. It is a supportive role, and the parties are primarily responsible and engaged with an eye to their own business needs and marketplace realities.

Every step of the way, they will still encounter the choice between conditioned, adversarial, enemy imagesorthemindsetof interdependence and cocreation, but with their Touchstone and ACED provisions, they will have awareness and the capacity to choose between coercion (violence) and collaboration (nonviolence).

> *Under ordinary circumstances, we shudder at the thought of behaving violently toward innocent people, even total strangers, and this is most likely a crucial feature of our moral brains.*
> *—Joshua Greene, Moral Tribes*

Research has demonstrated that our human capacity for empathy triggers in each of us a palpable, negative physical and neurological response to causing another person to suffer.[5]

---

[5] Cushman, Fiery, Kurt Gray, Allison Gaffey, and Wendy Berry Mendes. "Simulating Murder: The Aversion to Harmful Action." *Emotion* 12.1 (2012):

Studies have also shown that this aversion is specific to *performing the violent act oneself.* When performing the violent act is delegated or otherwise set at a distance from the initiator, the violence triggers less aversion.[6] I certainly have known times when a client demanded that I take actions or say and do coercive things to the other party that my client would not have been willing to do or say themselves. My client's aversion to violence was lessened—their capacity to initiate violence increased—by transferring to me, their lawyer, the responsibility for conducting the violence, making me the violent actor and the one to bear the consequences of the aversion response. It is my experience that by bringing the parties directly into the conflict conversation and returning to them the responsibility for choices made and implemented, Discovering Agreement encourages empathy and reduces the likelihood of coercive aggression—violence.

Catalyzing Change

"Self-help" programs that focus on improving the interior person but don't offer help for the student in taking action to catalyze change in the world at large often seem agonizingly slow—even inadequate—to affect the world's problems. The interior work of contemplation and growth, self-awareness, and self-mastery is obviously foundational and crucial, but it is not the complete story. I want activism, change-makers not just change-experiencers. *Applied spirituality* is what I want to see and be. Andrew Harvey talks about "sacred activism"[7] and maybe this is what he is getting at. For me, it has to do with merging the formerly separate paths of spirit and values on the one hand with so-called arm's length, hard-nosed business deals on the other. It

2–7.

[6] Ibid.

[7] "Sacred Activism | Spiritual Teaching | Author Andrew Harvey." *Andrew Harvey.* Institute for Sacred Activism, Web. 28 Aug. 2015.

involves more than just being the "wonderful" person in the group. When I say "be the change," I mean both hold tight to truth AND take action—productive, tested, challenging, can't-be-ignored action.

Ambient influence emanating from the "presence" of a person who is a shining example of enlightenment is—without a doubt—a great value, but how many of us are the Dalai Lama or Ram Dass? What chance is there that one or the other of us is going to achieve that level of presence and enlightenment in time for tomorrow's negotiation? To some extent, the dedicated spiritual seeker-practitioner will find that her/his presence and choices will achieve some effect, but the effect is subject to persistent and sometimes overwhelming back-pressure from cultural norms and the systems that have evolved to perpetuate those cultural norms.

I've always interpreted Gandhi's "be the change you wish to see in the world" statement to mean if you see that things need to change, the way to bring the change is not to wait for others, but to act, to exemplify the change you desire. For me it is a "do your bit no matter how small or ineffective" admonition. I also have understood it as a call for each of us to "walk our talk"—to live in integrity. Accepting that call and trying my best to be the change I want to see in the practice of law—practical application of my core values to daily client matters and work obligations—has led me to experience another, more subtle facet, of meaning in Gandhi's "walk your talk" statement. I've discovered that changing the way I am in the world is a vital and immediate way to actually trigger change.[8]

---

[8] According to his OpEd in the *New York Times,* Brian Morton made a concerted effort to confirm that Gandhi did, in fact, speak or write this famous phrase which is so often attributed to him. Mr. Morton concluded, *The closest verifiable remark we have from Gandhi is this: "If we could change ourselves, the tendencies in the world would also change. As a man changes his own nature, so does the attitude of the world change towards him....We need not wait to see what others do."* Morton, Brian. "Falser Words Were Never Spoken." *The New York Times.* The New York Times, 29 Aug. 2011. Web. 28

I believe we've all experienced this on a one-to-one level. Changing our tone or attitude can quickly and radically change a personal interaction (for better or worse). As the Dalai Lama posted on Facebook (I never thought I'd write *that*), "Anger cannot be overcome by anger. If someone is angry with you, and you show anger in return, the result is a disaster. On the other hand, if you control your anger and show its opposite—love, compassion, tolerance and patience—not only will you remain peaceful, but the other person's anger will also diminish." When I began practicing what I have come to call "applied integrity," I had not taken into account the fact that by changing the way I conduct myself and my conversations, I change the options available to others. My choice to act on different foundational principles caused others' unexamined assumptions to be illuminated and oftentimes dissolved.

Tool Kit

If I were to create a Discovering Agreement Tool Kit, I would have to include self-awareness and personal development tools such as meditation and mindfulness practices, but I would want more. I can't wait for my personal development to rise to the level of the Dalai Lama or Nelson Mandela. I have meetings and decisions and disputes and client matters to manage. What can I use to build my personal development strengths and also, at the same time, increase the likelihood that my business and legal interactions (with people and systems) will influence broader, deeper change? It is essential for meaningful, durable change that we not only address the personal, inner culture, but that we create alternative systems that support, sustain, and spread the change to the wider culture— business, community, and beyond. Pragmatic change, achievable by the yet-to-be-enlightened person through active engagement of the existing problem and system is the thing that interests me. Give me a frame of reference and give me a structural framework that together will keep me on track in the face of cultural conditioning, practices, systems, and norms. It is out of this need that the principles, the frame, and framework of DA developed.

DA offers a real, practical, viable alternative to our habitual, conventional models for managing business relationships. It enables the parties to create their own system for retaining power of self-determination, for problem solving—with greater efficiency and productivity than our current, conventional systems. It becomes a catalyst of change to the larger system by giving parties an alternative, nonadversarial way to powerfully engage conflict. Parties that experience the difference between a DA conversation and conventional contract formation, drafting, and enforcement want to apply the principles of DA to all of their agreements. In this way, the experience is shared and spread to an ever widening group, removing from the overburdened litigation system those conflicts that are more appropriately left in the hands of the parties (and the facilitators of nonadversarial conflict) and freeing parties from the costs in time and treasure that conventional conflict imposes.

Applying the Discovering Agreement Mindset in Daily Practice

Worry is defined as the contemplation of potentially dangerous situations and coping strategies, associated with problem solving to prevent danger.[9] What is more, "repetitive negative thinking is a feature of most types of psychological dysfunctions."[10] Lawyers are professional worriers. It is our job to watch out for

---

[9] Bahrami, Fatemeh, Rahim Kasaei, and Ahmadreza Zamani. "Preventing Worry and Rumination by Induced Positive Emotion." *International Journal of Preventative Medicine* 3.2 (2012): 102–09. Medknow Publications & Media Pvt Ltd. Web. 28 Aug. 2015.

[10] Ibid.

potential dangers and develop strategies to cope with or prevent the danger. When I believe that the world is full of adversaries and that conflict means battle, it is logical to see my job as aggressive, confrontational, and combative.

As a law student and lawyer, I was indoctrinated to the "hired gun" model—"zealous representation" meant getting the outcome my client demanded. I felt like I had to overpower every opponent, bending them to the will of my client. My job was to outargue, outmaneuver, and outwit everyone. I lived in fear and I lived by fear, wielding it as a weapon to drive others to do as I dictated. It was unbelievably distasteful and soul-killing, and I was really good at it. I was receiving kudos for being a top-notch paranoid-bully. I was a highly paid, terror-stricken terrorist for hire. I hated it but could see no alternative. Then two planes flew into the World Trade Center towers.

Integrity

I believe that integrity is the best, most reliable source of power. We think that domination is equivalent to power, but that sort of power is always in play, always under challenge, always in need of bolstering and defense. It is also always and ultimately vulnerable to and subverted by any individual who demonstrates unshakeable integrity.

What is this powerful force "integrity"?

Integrity is the alignment of actions with deeply held values and vision. If you know your values and your vision, you can hold to those as an unfailing navigational guide through all decisions and conflicts and collaborations and efforts. If you know your coparty's vision, mission, and values ("VMV")—and they know yours—then it will be much more likely that everyone can conduct the relationship and shared efforts in harmony, productively and with profound enjoyment. Integrity is rewarding, mentally, emotionally, spiritually, and quite often, financially. It is certainly easier to persevere through difficulties when your efforts are in alignment with deeply held and clearly formed VMV.

On the flip side, it can be terribly painful to fail to live up to your VMV. And it happens to each and every one of us, frequently. That is the "human condition." What redeems us is our dedication to renewed effort to live up to our VMV. You cannot do better than your best. And we are all doing our best. Trying is more worthwhile than not trying. After a stumble, it is easier to recover if one can reach for and locate one's VMV— the touchstone of integrity—to reorient the heart and mind and intention.

Can integrity be powerful in the face of a bully or systemized aggression? Ask Gandhi. Ask Dr. King. Ask Lech Walesa and Vàclav Havel. Ask Viktor Frankl. Ask me. Ask my clients.

Love as a Career Choice

> *The consummation of work lies not only in what we have done, but who we have become while accomplishing the task.*
> —David Whyte, Crossing the Unknown Sea:
> Work as a Pilgrimage of Identity

By the way I am doing my work, what am I becoming?

Not too long ago, I was asked to give a presentation at a career development conference for lawyers. The topic I was assigned was, "Building A Legal Career With Authenticity." Being a lawyer, the first thing I did was to look up the definition of "authentic" and I found it was "real, true, not copied or false." Then, I thought about the questions implicit in the title, "How do I live an authentic life in the context of my work as a lawyer?" and "How do I create a legal career that doesn't generate dissonance between my nature and my work?"

I find it fascinating that these are questions we need to ask ourselves. What about the practice of law is counter to our natural authenticity? I think part of the problem is that our profession seems to dictate a certain "way of being" and we assume that to deviate from that model is dangerous, irresponsible, and even impossible. Our legal training impresses upon us the primacy of rules and precedent. We are expected to separate emotion from action. The very role of the lawyer is to be supremely rational, fundamentally pessimistic, and demanding of perfection from ourselves and others.

In precedent we trust. We believe we must conform to the way things are done, even if our personal values (and common sense) are offended. Deviating from established practices is frowned upon. Too risky. And we know that lawyers are not allowed to make mistakes! We are trained to look to the past, to preserve consistency in service of predictability. This makes sense in terms of "stare decisis,"[11] but the primacy of convention and tradition tends to be applied to the whole of our legal life. Conformity becomes a value and nonconformity a taboo.

"Feelings" are equivalent to vulnerability. We equate vulnerability with weakness and exposure to harm. Implicit in our training is the imperative to overcome our feelings, to set them aside when making decisions. Emotions cannot be trusted. They tend to run away with people and can lead to irrational behavior. Lawyers are asked to engage and be rational in life's most painful and paradoxical circumstances; hence, we expect ourselves to partition our hearts from our work.

The reality is that the heart has power that will manifest even if you believe you have blocked its influence. Lawyers have disproportionately high rates of depression, substance abuse, burnout, divorce, and suicide. The question that presents itself is, how can we engage the power of the heart and still be effective lawyers who are credible and successful (professionally, financially, and personally)? Can we follow our heart and still

---

[11] Courts cite to *stare decisis* when an issue has been previously brought to the court and a ruling already issued. "Stare Decisis." Legal Information Institute Cornell Law School, Web. 28 Aug. 2015.

pay off our student loans?

If we don't want the heart to take a subversive role in our lives, then we need to find a way to work with it, to harness its power for our own good, for the good of those we love, and for the good of the world. Know your own heart and align with it. Anxiety, depression, and burnout are signals of misalignment.

I'm not suggesting that we just start allowing unease or discomfort to call the shots or capriciously "follow our bliss." I am suggesting that we get really familiar with what is calling the shots and then decide if that is what we want governing our decisions—get really familiar with what truly exerts on us a magnetic force, exciting our energies and passions.

For many of us, the expectations of family and culture have a strong influence on our decision making. But we rarely take a clear-eyed look at just exactly what those expectations are, and whether those expectations make sense to us and the life we want to lead.

The one thing over which you have complete control is your personal integrity. There will be times when others have the power to take away your money, your job, your freedom, even your life, but they can never take away your personal integrity. Personal integrity is yours. You can sell it. You can give it away. Or you can keep it. Integrity is the true seat of power in every life.

Articulate your own personal lodestar for navigating decisions and crises. Provide yourself with a reminder that orients you to your core truths, your whole-hearted truth; then you can answer challenges with positive, creative exploration rather than reactiveness. Then, you won't have to wonder whether a decision is right or wrong. You don't have to wonder how to measure its virtues or faults. All you have to do is check to see whether it is in alignment with your deeply held values, whether it violates your core constraints and imperatives, and whether it serves your vision and furthers your mission.

Conscious awareness of the governing principles of your life and career, the deep values that your heart holds—sometimes in spite of your intellect and the expectations of others—is the foundation of your personal power. That awareness continually aligns you and realigns you with your personal integrity, helping you stay connected with and in the flow of the greater source of power—your autonomy—your ability to choose your own responses rather than being the unwitting victim of manipulation, emotional or otherwise. Even if you decide to accept a course of action that some other has engineered for you through coercive means, or that does not fully align with your vision, mission, and values, you do it with consciousness, alert to the risk to your integrity and alert to the risk of backlash.

If finances and the expectations of others govern your choices, you take a great risk—the risk that you will create a life you do not love, that does not match your true nature, and that demands of you a falseness and smallness unworthy of the potential you embody. It is when we are focused on meeting our highest level of needs (self-actualization), the decisions we make and actions we take are far more likely to gather to us the resources to meet and satisfy lower-level needs (food, shelter, paying off student loans).[12]

> *Don't aim at success. The more you aim at it and make it a target, the more you are going to miss it. For success, like happiness, cannot be pursued; it must ensue, and it only does so as the unintended side effect of one's personal dedication to a cause greater than oneself...Happiness must happen, and the same holds for success: you have to let it happen by not caring about it. I want you to listen to what your conscience commands you to do and go on to carry it out to the*

---

[12] Kay, J. A. *Obliquity: Why Our Goals Are Best Achieved Indirectly.* New York: Penguin, 2011. Print.; Kay, John A. "TEDxWarwick John Kay Obliquity: How Complex Goals Are Best Achieved Indirectly." *YouTube.* TEDx, 22 Mar. 2012. Web. 28 Aug. 2015.

best of your knowledge. Then you will live to see that in the long-run—in the long-run, I say!—success will follow you precisely because you had forgotten to think about it.

—Viktor E. Frankl, Man's Search for Meaning

Building a legal career with authenticity is a practice of satyagraha— holding to the truth, your truth.

What Really Matters Is Expressing Love

On September 11, 2001, the calls that were made from the Twin Towers were not about "why me?" or rage, or revenge, or blame. All the calls were to tell others, "I love you." Those people who knew they were in their last moments wanted only to have a last opportunity to express love.

In work, expressing love is bringing something of value and meaning to the world. Your legal career is an expression of your true self. It can be an expression of love if you choose.

I dare you.

Works Cited

"Agile Methodology Understanding Agile Methodology." *Agile Methodology* RSS.Web. 25 Aug. 2015.

Anders, George. "Gurus Gone Wild: Does Zappos' Reorganization Make Any Sense?" *Forbes*. Forbes Magazine, 9 Jan. 2014.

"Apple Open Source." *Apple - Open Source*. Web. 25 Aug. 2015. <http://www.apple.com/opensource/>.

Arnold, Kyle. "Posts." *Reflective Listening: Rogers' Paradox*. Saybrook University, 4 June 2015. Web. 28 Aug. 2015.

Bahrami, Fatemeh, Rahim Kasaei, and Ahmadreza Zamani. "Preventing Worry and Rumination by Induced Positive Emotion." *International Journal of Preventative Medicine* 3.2 (2012): 102–09. Medknow Publications & Media Pvt Ltd. Web. 28 Aug. 2015.

Barter, Dominic. "DominicBarterJune12015." *SoundCloud*. Keynote Address, Nat'l Assoc. of Community and Restorative Justice, 1 June 2015. Web. 25 Aug. 2015.

Barter, Dominic. "An Introduction to Restorative Circles with Dominic Barter." Vimeo. Https://vimeo.com/user2006 436, 2010. Web. 23 Aug. 2015. for in-formation: www.restorativecircles.org

Berfield, Susan. "Container Store: Conscious Capitalism and the Perils of Going Public." *Bloomberg.com*. Bloomberg Businessweek, 19 Feb. 2015.

Biography: Ben and Jerry. By Amy Martinez. Perf. Liz Bankowski, Ben Cohen, Zak Fine. 2006. TV Episode.

Boldren, Michele, and David K. Levine. "Open-Source Software: Who Needs Intellectual Property? |

Foundation for Economic Education." *FEE Freeman Article*. Foundation for Economic Education, 1 Jan. 2007.

Bollier, David. "The Commons as a New | Old Paradigm for Governance, Economics and Policy – Part One." *Kosmos Journal*. 2013. Web. 25 Aug. 2015. <paradigm-for-governance-economics-and-policy-part-one/>.

Bollier, David. "The New Economic Events Giving Lie to the Fiction That We Are All Selfish, Rational Materialists." *Alternet*. Independent Media Institute, 14 Apr. 2014.

Chrisman, P. Oswin, Gay G. Cox, and Petra Novotna. "Collaborative Practice Mediation: Are We Ready to Serve This Emerging Market." *Pepperdine Dispute Resolution Law Journal* 6.3 (2006): 451–64.

Collins, James C. *Good to Great: Why Some Companies Make the Leap–and Others Don't*. New York, NY: Harper Business, 2001. Print.

Conley, Chip. "Chapter Ten: Creating Trust." *Peak: How Great Companies Get Their Mojo from Maslow*. 1st ed. San Francisco: Jossey-Bass, 2007. 171–87. Print.

"Conscious Contracts." *www.consciouscontracts.com* Web. 28 Aug. 2015.

Covey, Stephen M. R., and Rebecca R. Merrill. *The Speed of Trust: The One Thing That Changes Everything*. New York: Free Press, 2008. Print.

Covey, Stephen R., and Breck England. *The 3rd Alternative: Solving Life's Most Difficult Problems*. New York: Free Press, 2011. Print.

Crosby, Michelle. "Peace Provoking An Oxymoron?" *Life: Wevorce*. Wevorce, 3 Aug. 2013. Web. 27 Aug. 2015.

Cushman, Fiery, Kurt Gray, Allison Gaffey, and Wendy Berry Mendes. "Simulating Murder: The Aversion to Harmful Action." *Emotion* 12.1 (2012): 2–7.

"Cutting Edge Law.com." *www.Cutting Edge Law.com*. Web. 28 Aug. 2015.

De Vries, Berend R., and Maurits Barendrecht. "Fitting the Forum to the Fuss with Sticky Defaults: Failure in the Market for Dispute Resolution Services?" *Cardozo Journal of Conflict Resolution* 7.1 (2006).

Denning, Steve. "Making Sense of Zappos and Holacracy." *Forbes*. Forbes Magazine, 15 Jan. 2014.

"The Efficiency of Trust: Capacity Building for Effective Change." *YouTube*. MEL Talks at Meliora Weekend 2014, 13 Mar. 2015. Web. 28 Aug. 2015. Featuring Kit Miller, Director of the M.K. Gandhi Institute for Nonviolence.

Eknath, Easwaran, and Michael N. Nagler. "The Unity of Life." *The Upanishads*. Tomales, CA: Nilgiri, 2007. 265–67. Print.

Elliott, Stuart. "Selling Products by Selling Shared Values." *The New York Times*. The New York Times, 13 Feb. 2013. Web. 25 Aug. 2015. <http://www.nytimes.com/2013/02/14/business/media/panera-to-advertise-its-social-consciousness-advertising.html>.

Fisher, Roger, and Daniel Shapiro. *Beyond Reason: Using Emotions as You Negotiate*. New York: Viking, 2005. Print.

Fisher, Roger, and William Ury. *Getting to Yes: Negotiating an Agreement without Giving in*. London: Random House Business, 2012. Print.

Frankl, Viktor E. *Man's Search for Meaning*. New York: Washington Square/ Pocket, 1985. Print.

Friedman, Gary J., and Jack Himmelstein. *Challenging Conflict: Mediation through Understanding*. Chicago, IL: American Bar Association, 2008. Print.

Fryer, Bronwyn. "The Rise of Compassionate Management (Finally)." *Harvard Business Review*. Harvard Business Publishing, 18 Sept. 2013.

Gandhi, and Thomas Merton. "Section Two, Non-Violence: True and False." *Gandhi on Non-violence: Selected Texts from Mohandas K. Gandhi's Nonviolence in Peace and War.* New York: New Directions Pub., 2007. 50. Print.

Gandhi. *Non-violence in Peace & War.* Vol. 1. Ahmedabad: Navajivan, 1944. Print.

Gilbert, Alison. "Social Media and Hurricane Sandy." *Digital Ethos.* 15 Nov. 2012.

Gillies, Peter S., and Andrew Dahdal. "Waiver of a Right to Arbitrate by Resort to Litigation, in the Context of International Commercial Arbitration." *Journal of International Commercial Law and Technology* 2.4 (2007): 221–30.

Goleman, Daniel. *Emotional Intelligence: Why It Can Matter More than IQ: & Working with Emotional Intelligence.* London: Bloomsbury, 2004. Print.

Greene, Joshua David. *Moral Tribes: Emotion, Reason, and the Gap between Us and Them.* 1st ed. New York: Penguin, 2013. Print.

Greene, Joshua David. *Moral Tribes: Emotion, Reason, and the Gap between Us and Them.* : Penguin, 2014. Print.

Hindle, Tim. *Guide to Management Ideas and Gurus.* London: Profile, 2008. Print.

"The Holes in Holacracy." *The Economist.* The Economist Newspaper, 05 July 2014.

Homes, Oliver Wendell, Jr. "The Path of the Law." *Harvard Law Review* 10 (1897): 460–61.

Howard, Phillip K. "Four Ways to Fix a Broken Legal System." *Philip K. Howard:.*TED, Feb. 2010. Web. 24 Aug. 2015.

Hsieh, Tony. *Delivering Happiness: A Path to Profits, Passion, and Purpose.* New York: Grand Central, 2010. Print.

The Internet of Things Meets the Internet of People Infinite Interactions Drives New Values. : Harbor Research, 2010. PDF. Web. 25 Aug. 2015.

Johnson, M. Alex. "Humans of New York Raises $2 Million to End Forced Labor in Pakistan." *NBC News.* 19 Aug. 2015. Web. 25 Aug. 2015.

Kanter, Rosabeth Moss. "How Great Companies Think Differently." *Harvard Business Review*. Harvard Business Publishing, 01 Nov. 2011. Web. 25 Aug. 2015.

Kay, J. A. *Obliquity: Why Our Goals Are Best Achieved Indirectly*. New York: Penguin, 2011. Print.

Kay, John A. "TEDxWarwick John Kay Obliquity: How Complex Goals Are Best Achieved Indirectly." *YouTube*. TEDx, 22 Mar. 2012. Web. 28 Aug. 2015.

King, Jeff, and Jeff Fromm. "Only Conscious Capitalists Will Survive." *Forbes*. Forbes Magazine, 4 Dec. 2013.

Kofman, Fred. *Conscious Business: How to Build Value through Values*. Boulder, CO: Sounds True, 2006. Print.

Kofman, Fred. *Conscious Business*. Rec. 1 Sept. 2006. Sounds True, 2006. CD.

Laloux, Frederic. *Reinventing Organizations: A Guide to Creating Organizations Inspired by the Next Stage of Human Consciousness*. Brussels, Belgium: Nelson Parker, 2014. Print.

Lamm, Claus, C. Daniel Batson, and Jean Decety. "The Neural Substrate of Human Empathy: Effects of Perspective-taking and Cognitive Appraisal." *Journal of Cognitive Neuroscience* 19.1 (2007): 42–58.

Lamott, Anne. *Crooked Little Heart*. New York: Pantheon, 1997. Print.

"Law Firm Hours – The Real Story." *Above the Law*. Lateral Link, 24 July 2012. Web. 27 Aug. 2015.

Levine, Stewart. *The Book of Agreement*. San Francisco, CA: Berrett-Koehler, 2002. Print.

Levine, Stewart. *Getting to Resolution: Turning Conflict into Collaboration*. San Francisco, CA: Berrett-Koehler, 2009. Print.

Levine, Stewart. "Resolutionary View: 10 Principles for Developing the Attitude of Resolution." *Law Practice Today* (2006): Web. ABA Law Practice Management Section.

Liberman, V. "The Name of the Game: Predictive Power of Reputations versus Situational Labels in Determining Prisoner's Dilemma Game Moves." *Personality and Social Psychology Bulletin* 30.9 (2004): 1175–185.

McGrath, Rita. "Failing by Design." *Harvard Business Review.* 01 Apr. 2011.

Mnookin, Robert H., Scott R. Peppet, and Andrew S. Tulumello. *Beyond Winning: Negotiating to Create Value in Deals and Disputes.* Cambridge, MA: Belknap of Harvard UP, 2000. Print.

Montanaro, Dominico. "Indiana Law: Sorting Fact from Fiction from Politics." *NPR.* NPR, 1 Apr. 2015. Web. 25 Aug. 2015.

Morin, Amy. "Introducing a Little Compassion to Your Workplace Culture Has Big Benefits." *Forbes.* Forbes Magazine, 24 June 2015.

Morton, Brian. "Falser Words Were Never Spoken." *The New York Times.* The New York Times, 29 Aug. 2011.

Nagler, Michael N. *The Nonviolence Handbook: A Guide for Practical Action.* San Francisco, CA: Berrett-Koehler, 2014. Print.

O'Donohue, John. "Towards a Poetics of Possibility." *An Easter People: Essays in Honour of Sr Stanislaus Kennedy.* Ed. John Scally. Dublin, Ireland: Veritas, 2005. Print.

Peck, M. Scott. *In Search of Stones: A Pilgrimage of Faith, Reason, and Discovery.* New York: Hyperion, 1995. Print.

Peter M. Senge. Society for Organizational Learning, North America, Web. 28 Aug. 2015.

Pranis, Kay. *The Little Book of Circle Processes: A New/Old Approach to Peacemaking.* Intercourse, PA: Good, 2005. Print.

Rifkin, Jeremy. *The Zero Marginal Cost Society: The Internet of Things, the Collaborative Commons, and the Eclipse of Capitalism.* New York: Palgrave/ Macmillan, 2014.

135–51. Print.

Robertson, Brian J. *Holacracy: The New Management System for a Rapidly Changing World.* Henry Holt, 2015. Print.

"Sacred Activism | Spiritual Teaching | Author Andrew Harvey." *Andrew Harvey.* Institute for Sacred Activism, Web. 28 Aug. 2015.

Satell, Greg. "Managing For Disruption." *Forbes.* Forbes Magazine, 13 Mar. 2014.

Schwartz, Barry, and Kenneth Sharpe. *Practical Wisdom: The Right Way to Do the Right Thing.* 1st ed. New York: Riverhead, 2010. Print.

Schwartz,Tony."CompaniesThatPractice'ConsciousCapitalism'Perform10xBetter." *Harvard Business Review.* 04 Apr. 2013. Web. 25 Aug. 2015. <https://hbr.org/2013/04/companies-that-practice-conscious-capitalism-perform>.

Senge, Peter M. *The Fifth Discipline: The Art and Practice of the Learning Organization.* New York: Doubleday/Currency, 2006. Print.

Sinek, Simon. *Start with Why: How Great Leaders Inspire Everyone to Take Action.* New York: Portfolio, 2009. Print.

Sisodia, Rajendra, Jagdish N. Sheth, and David B. Wolfe. *Firms of Endearment: How World-class Companies Profit from Passion and Purpose.* 2nd ed. New Jersey: Pearson Education, 2014. Print.

Sklar, Charlotte. "ALTERNATIVE COURTS IN TRIBAL COMMUNITIES." Ed. Michelle Rivard Parks. *2d Annual Peacemakers Gathering: Preserving Tribal Justice through Indigenous Peacemaking, Executive Summary* (2008): Appendix.

"Social Media and Hurricanes What We've Learned Since Sandy." *Social Media and Hurricanes What We've Learned Since Sandy.* Homeland Security Science and Technology, Web. 25 Aug. 2015.

Soukhanov, Anne H. *Microsoft Encarta College Dictionary.*

New York: St. Martin's, 2001. Print.

"Stare Decisis." *Stare Decisis.* Legal Information Institute Cornell Law School, Web. 28 Aug. 2015.

"Triple Bottom Line." *The Economist.* The Economist Newspaper, 17 Nov. 2009. Web. 27 Aug. 2015. (article adapted from "The Economist Guide to Management Ideas and Gurus", Hindle, Tim. London: Profile, 2008. Print).

"TriplePundit: Reporting on the Triple Bottom Line & Sustainable Business News." *Triple Pundit People Planet Profit.* Triple Pundit, LLC., Web. 27 Aug. 2015.

Ury, William, Jeanne M. Brett, and Stephen B. Goldberg. *Getting Disputes Resolved: Designing Systems to Cut the Costs of Conflict.* San Francisco: JosseyBass, 1988. Print.

Ury, William. *The Power of a Positive No: How to Say No and Still Get to Yes.* New York: Bantam, 2007. Print.

Wall, Derek. *The Commons in History: Culture, Conflict, and Ecology.* Cambridge, Mass: MIT, 2014. Print.

Wall, Matthew. "Innovate or Die: The Stark Message for Big Business BBC News." *BBC News.* BBC News Services, 5 Sept. 2014.

"What Is the Difference between a Benefit Corporation and a B Corp? Cutting Edge Capital." *Cutting Edge Capital.* 28 May 2013. Web. 27 Aug. 2015.

"Why Fostering a Culture of Compassion in the Workplace Matters–K@W." *KnowledgeWharton Why Fostering a Culture of Companionate Love in the Workplace Matters Comments.* Wharton School of the University of Pennsylvania, 2 Apr. 2014.

Wright, J. Kim. "Conscious Contracts: Bringing Purpose and Values into Legal Documents." Web log post. *Jkimwright.com.* 30 July 2015. Web. 28 July 2015.

Wright, J. Kim. *Lawyers as Peacemakers: Practicing Holistic, Problem-solving Law.* Chicago, IL: American Bar

Association, 2010. Print.

Yazzie, The Honorable Robert. "Life Comes from It: Navajo Justice Concepts." *New Mexico Law Review* Spring. 24 (1994): 175.

"Yes, You Can Make Money with Open Source." *Harvard Business Review*. 15 Jan. 2013.

Zender, Tom. "Discover the Power of Consciousness in Your Business Phoenix Business Journal." *Phoenix Business Journal*. 2 Jan. 2015. Web. 25 Aug. 2015. <the-power-of-consciousness-in-your.html>.

Zhu, Dengya, Vidyasagar Potdar, and Elizabeth Chang. "Open Source Software Development (OSSD) Based On Software Engineering." *IFIP International Federation for Information Processing Open Source Systems* (2006): 345–46. Web. 25 Aug. 2015. <http://floss hub.org/system/files/potdar106-110.pdf>.

Appendix: Samples and Examples

I felt some hesitation about including samples and examples of Discovering Agreement (DA) documents in this book, especially ACED provisions. It can be very tempting to just drop a provision from the last document one drafted into the next that is being created for another client. When I have this impulse, I remind myself how crucial it is that the people who will be depending on the system are truly invested in its successful implementation. This buy-in comes, in large part, from the parties being the owners of their conflict process through meaningful participation in choosing or designing the structure they will use when tensions rise or anger erupts. *Resist the urge to copy and paste.*

With that caveat, what follows are samples and examples of various DA provisions as used in different situations and types of contracts. Where necessary to protect privacy or confidentiality, details and other identifying information have been changed or deleted. Some of the examples are from agreements I have worked on, others are adapted from agreements or materials other practicing attorneys have shared with me.

While most of the samples provided here are from agreements where the parties are either individuals or smaller businesses, DA provisions can be used easily and seamlessly in larger, more complex contract documents and contractual relationships.

Excerpts from Linda's Engagement Letter Form

Linda's Touchstone Statement

Vision—I envision a world where the power of love has replaced the love of power. This vision includes a legal system that inspires and supports sustainable, beneficial, regenerative behaviors, relationships, and enterprises—a system that allows individuals, organizations, and communities to conduct all their legal affairs in alignment with their values, their principles, and their vision for a better world.

Mission—My mission is to support clients in conducting their legal affairs in alignment with their values, their principles, and their vision for a better world and to conduct myself and my practice in a way that stimulates and sustains positive effects—social, environmental, financial, and personal—for my clients, for myself, and for all beings (family, friends, colleagues, our local and global communities, and future generations).

Principles & Values—In service of my vision and mission, I choose to practice in accordance with the following principles and values:

- winning does not require a loser;
- safety is mutual or it is not real safety;[1]
- finding ways to join forces with others and—together—design sustainable, beneficial, and enjoyable relationships and enterprises is better than approaching deal-making as an encounter between

---

[1] "Safety" as used here means having sufficient predictability, so that one's expectations are reasonably assured, enabling one to plan and venture with well-founded confidence that one will retain the power to take a meaningful role in responding to changing circumstances and will have an equal voice and be treated fairly should conflict arise.

opposing forces seeking to win an advantage, one over the other;

- addressing conflict and crisis need not involve coercion or manipulation.

I expect clients to gladly take an active, fully engaged role designing and conducting each deal/relationship/undertaking in which they engage.

I provide to my clients information and analysis on how the law and current legal system might affect their potential deal/relationship/undertaking/conflict and how to best put into words the terms and conditions of the agreements they reach with others, so that the existing system is most likely to support and protect everyone's intentions and expectations.

I value honesty, reliability, excellence, responsiveness, kindness, and enjoyment. I believe that integrity (consciously aligning one's actions with one's deeply held values) is the cornerstone of any worthwhile endeavor. Each person acting in integrity and taking responsibility for his or her own actions and desires is key to my enjoyment and willingness to work with anyone. I value honest communication and striving for clarity even when it is uncomfortable. When it comes to both personal and professional behavior, I believe the best guide is the Golden Rule.

Touchstone Statement of [ ]:

Please provide me with a statement of your Vision, Mission and Principles & Values for our work together as lawyer and client so that we can include it in this document. For your reference, should you wish to use them, I have attached a set of questions designed to spark creativity in thinking about and drafting your Vision-Mission-Values statement.

Addressing Change & Engaging Disagreement

We each understand that it is possible there will be occurrences that no one anticipated. It is also possible that times may come when we find ourselves in disagreement over some aspect of our relationship or the work related to this Engagement. If something unanticipated happens or if we find ourselves in disagreement, each of us is committed to avoiding adversarial proceedings of any kind and to collaborating to cocreate whatever transformation will best serve the needs of all.

Informal Conversation. Accordingly, if we find ourselves in disagreement, we each commit to dedicate our efforts towards bringing ourselves back into agreement as quickly as possible by talking together (in person or by videoconference) honestly, openly, in good faith, and with a commitment to finding a way forward that accords with and is in service of the Touchstones we've stated above.

The party who feels the need to call an informal conversation for this purpose will begin by providing to the other party a brief statement of the event/action/inaction that has triggered the request for the conversation, a statement of whether (and why) the event/action/inaction appears to be out of alignment with one or both stated Touchstone(s) or other terms of this Engagement Letter, and suggest a time for the conversation.

We'll open any such conversation by first reading the following reminder,

The Touchstone statements in our Engagement Agreement express our core, underlying interests in connection with this attorney/client relationship. They represent the vision(s) we hold that motivate us to persevere in our work, the mission(s) we are joining forces to accomplish, the principles, constraints and imperatives that inform our decision making, and the values with which we want to align all our actions.

The Touchstone statements are meant to serve as reference points to orient and focus our conversations in support of creative, productive, and collaborative problem solving should we find ourselves in disagreement in the course of our relationship and work together.

and then rereading together the Touchstones stated in this Engagement Letter.

We will focus our dialogue[2] on brainstorming ways to bring ourselves and our actions back into alignment with the stated Touchstones that work for both of us, beginning by asking ourselves the following questions:

1. What do we most appreciate about the work we have done together so far?
2. Are there outside influences (or money) affecting how we are working together?
3. Does each of us feel we are getting what we anticipated? Is there something that is no longer working for one or both of us?
4. What has really worked well for us so far? How can we expand on it?
5. Is it time to redefine or redirect our work together?
6. Is there something difficult we are avoiding saying or doing?
7. What do we gain by continuing/ending this work together?

Mediation. If we find that we are unable to design resolution amongst ourselves by informal discussion conducted in accordance with the Values and focused on serving the Vision and Mission as stated above, then we agree to attempt to resolve any dispute, claim or controversy arising out of or relating to this Statement of Agreement by mediation, which shall be conducted under the then current mediation procedures of *The Center for Understanding in Conflict*[3] or any other joint-session mediation

---

[2] By "dialogue" we mean, a person-to-person conversation with no preconceived outcome, listening not to refute but to comprehend one another's meaning, and with a willingness to be influenced and changed by what we hear.
[3] This joint-session, interest-based mediation approach developed by Gary Friedman and Jack Himmelstein is my preferred, designated backup system for

procedure upon which we may agree at that time.

We further agree that our respective good faith participation in mediation (or collaborative-style dispute resolution) is a condition precedent to pursuing any other available legal or equitable remedy, including litigation, arbitration, or other dispute resolution procedures.

Any one of us may commence the mediation/collaborative process by providing to the other written notice, setting forth the subject of the dispute, claim, or controversy and the relief requested. Within ten (10) calendar days after the receipt of the foregoing notice, each recipient shall deliver a written response to the sender. The initial mediation/collaborative session shall be held within thirty (30) calendar days after the initial notice.

We agree to share equally the costs and expenses of the mediation/ collaborative process (which shall not include the expenses incurred by each party for its own legal representation in connection with the mediation).

We further acknowledge and agree that mediation/ collaborative proceedings are settlement negotiations, and that, to the extent allowed by applicable law, all offers, promises, conduct, and statements, whether oral or written, made in the course of the mediation by any of the parties or our agents shall be confidential and inadmissible in any arbitration or other legal proceeding involving the parties; provided, however, that evidence, which is otherwise admissible or discoverable, shall not be rendered inadmissible or nondiscoverable as a result of its use in the mediation/collaborative process.

The provisions of this section may be enforced by any Court of competent jurisdiction, and the party seeking enforcement

---

Discovering Agreement parties as it is, in my opinion, closely aligned with the principles and values that I hold for Discovering Agreement. For information about the model and trainings: http://www.understandinginconflict.org/about/ our-history/; Friedman, Gary J., and Jack Himmelstein. *Challenging Conflict: Mediation through Understanding.* Chicago, IL: American Bar Association, 2008. Print.

shall be entitled to an award of all costs, fees, and expenses, including reasonable attorneys' fees, to be paid by the party against whom enforcement is ordered.

An alternative "do-it-yourself " system for productive conflict that some parties have adopted is Stewart Levine's "Getting to Resolution" process as described in his book of that title.[4] When parties have chosen Stewart's process for their backup (in case informal talks are not sufficient), I've used the following language in their Statement of Agreement,

> "If we find that we are unable to reach resolution between ourselves, we agree to use Stewart Levine's "Resolution Model" to reach agreement (found in his book entitled "Getting to Resolution" ISBN-13: 978-1576757710)."

And if the parties prefer not to name a particular mediation or mediator, I have used,

> "If we are not able to make significant progress towards resolution on our own after two meetings of at least one hour each using the Resolution Method, we agree that we will seek the assistance of a professional collaborative communications specialist or a professional mediator (and to share the costs of hiring that professional 50/50—which shall not include the expenses incurred by each party for its own legal representation in connection with the facilitated/mediated conversation)."

---

[4] Levine, Stewart. *Getting to Resolution: Turning Conflict into Collaboration.* San Francisco, CA: Berrett-Koehler, 2009. Print.

Questions to spark creativity and thinking about Vision, Mission, and Values for the attorney/client relationship:

- What is my personal vision of a better world and how will this attorney/client relationship serve that vision?
- What assumptions am I holding that are key to my desire to seek the help of an attorney?
- What do I believe are key ingredients for a successful attorney/ client relationship?
- What do I believe are key ingredients for a successful collaboration of any kind?
- When have I been most satisfied with an attorney and why?
- When have I been most satisfied with a collaboration? A business relationship?—and why?

My Vision, Mission, and Values statement for the attorney/ client relationship:

Vision—A statement about why you do what you do, and about the world you'd like to be part of creating.

Mission—A statement about the specific purpose for which you want the help of an attorney—what do you hope to achieve with my help?

Values and Guiding Principles—A statement about what sorts of behaviors and basic principles are really important to you—essential for a healthy, enjoyable, productive working relationship.

Client intake questionnaire:[5]

[5] Example of some questions explored when considering or entering a new

1. Does your organization have a statement of Purpose or Mission, Vision, and Values? If so, what is it? (If not, there is some work to do to create this.)
2. How aligned with the statement (would you say) is the actual operation of your business? 1 to 10, with 10 being completely aligned. _____
3. What is your biggest challenge about staying aligned with this statement?
4. Have you been asked to deviate from your Purpose/Mission/Vision/Values in the past? How did you address that? How did the relationship go?
5. What will you not do for any price?

Regarding a specific deal that you're considering:

1. Who are the stakeholders in this transaction?
2. Do you know the Purpose or Vision/Mission/Values (VMV) of the other party or parties?
3. How does entering this agreement, conducting this transaction, move your VMV forward?

Conflict style:

1. What is your usual response to conflict? (For example, some people avoid it, some try to smooth things over, some instigate or escalate conflict, and others look for ways to compromise.)
2. How would you like to engage conflict?
3. What terms have you already worked out for this agreement?
4. What terms would you like to work out?
5. What else do I need to know about this transaction or relationship?

---

engagement, adapted from materials provided by J. Kim Wright.

Example of How Discovering Agreement Provisions Fit within Full Statement of Agreement

Statement of Agreement by and between G and L

L is assisting an author to publish his book titled, GREAT BOOK TITLE.

G has agreed to do a copy edit on the manuscript ("the Project").

G and L agree to the following terms and conditions:

Independent Contractor Status

G is an independent contractor, not L's employee. G and L agree to the following rights consistent with an independent contractor relationship: G has the right to perform services for others during the term of this Statement of Agreement.

G has the sole right to control and direct the means, manner, and method by which the services required by this Statement of Agreement are performed.

Intellectual Property

G hereby assigns to L all copyrights in and to any works created or developed by her for the book under this Statement of Agreement ("Work Product"). This assignment is conditioned upon full payment of the compensation due to G under this Statement of Agreement.

G will help prepare any documents L considers necessary to secure any copyright or other intellectual property rights in G's Work Product under this Statement of Agreement.

Compensation

G shall be paid $PLENTY/hour for her services on the Project.

G will invoice L on the first of each month or as soon as the project is completed—whichever is sooner.

Payment shall be due within 30 days of the date of G's invoice, or within 7 calendar days of when L receives payment from the author for the Work Product, whichever is sooner.

Local, State, and Federal Taxes

G shall pay all income taxes and FICA (Social Security and Medicare taxes) incurred while performing services under this Statement of Agreement. L will not:

- withhold FICA from G's payments or make FICA payments on L's behalf;
- make state or federal unemployment compensation contributions on G's behalf; or
- withhold state or federal income tax from G's payments.

Date of This Agreement and Termination

The date of this agreement will be the first e-mail date on the e-mail string in which L and G have both indicated their approval of this agreement. The agreement will continue in force until either L or G decides to terminate it. Termination requires no advance notice.

If L decides to terminate this agreement, she will promptly notify G via e-mail. If G decides to terminate this agreement, she will promptly notify L via e-mail. In either case, e-mail notification is considered notification in writing for the purposes of this Agreement. G and L are each responsible for keeping the other up to date on their appropriate e-mail address for this and all other notices.

Upon termination, G shall deliver to L all Work Product in whatever stage of completion it exists at the time of termination. Upon termination, G shall deliver to L a final invoice for work done by G up to the time of termination for payment in accordance with the Compensation provision of this Statement of Agreement.

Addressing Change and Engaging Disagreement

Both G and L understand that it is possible there will be occurrences that no one anticipated. It is also possible that times may come when we find ourselves in disagreement over some aspect of our relationship or the work related to this Statement of Agreement. If something unanticipated happens or if we find ourselves in disagreement, both L and G are committed to avoiding adversarial proceedings of any kind and to seeking instead a system for collaborating to bring whatever transformation will best serve the needs of all.

Accordingly, if we find ourselves in disagreement, we each commit to dedicate our efforts towards bringing ourselves back into agreement as quickly as possible by talking together honestly, openly, in good faith, and with a commitment to finding a way forward that will work for both of us.

We'll open any such conversation by asking ourselves the following questions:

1. What do we most appreciate about the work we have done together so far?
2. Are there outside influences (or money) affecting how we are working together?
3. Do each of us feel we are getting what we anticipated? Is there something that is no longer working for one or both of us?

4. What has really worked well for us so far? How can we expand on it?
5. Is it time to redefine or redirect our work together?
6. Is there something difficult we are avoiding saying or doing?
7. What do we gain by continuing/ending this work together?

We agree that if we find that we are unable to reach resolution among ourselves by informal discussion, then we agree to attempt to resolve any dispute, claim or controversy arising out of or relating to this Statement of Agreement by mediation, which shall be conducted under the then current mediation procedures of *The Center for Understanding in Conflict* or any other joint-session mediation procedure upon which we may agree at that time.

We also agree that good faith participation in mediation is a precondition to pursuing any other available legal or equitable remedy, including litigation, arbitration or other dispute resolution procedures.

1. Either party may commence the mediation process by providing to the other party written notice, setting forth the subject of the dispute, claim or controversy and the relief requested. Within ten (10) days after the receipt of the foregoing notice, the other party shall deliver a written response to the initiating party's notice.
2. The initial mediation session shall be held within thirty (30) days after the initial notice. The parties agree to share equally the costs and expenses of the mediation (which shall not include the expenses incurred by each party for its own legal representation in connection with the mediation).
3. The parties further acknowledge and agree that mediation proceedings are settlement negotiations, and

that, to the extent allowed by applicable law, all offers, promises, conduct, and statements, whether oral or written, made in the course of the mediation by any of the parties or their agents shall be confidential and inadmissible in any arbitration or other legal proceeding involving the parties; provided, however, that evidence which is otherwise admissible or discoverable shall not be rendered inadmissible or nondiscoverable as a result of its use in the mediation.

The provisions of this *Addressing Change and Engaging Disagreement* section shall survive termination of this Statement of Agreement and may be enforced by any Court of competent jurisdiction, and the party seeking enforcement shall be entitled to an award of all costs, fees, and expenses, including reasonable attorneys' fees, to be paid by the party against whom enforcement is ordered.

Entire Statement of Agreement

This Statement of Agreement contains the entire understanding between L and G. It shall be binding upon and inure to the benefit of L's and G's respective heirs, executors, administrators, representatives, and assigns. No promises, representation, or inducement, oral or written, have been made except as expressly set forth herein. In resolving any dispute or construing any provision hereunder, there shall be no presumptions made or inferences drawn because the attorneys for one party drafted this Statement of Agreement. This Statement of Agreement may be amended or modified only in writing signed by both L and G. No waiver of any breach of any provision of this Statement of Agreement shall constitute a waiver of any prior, concurrent or subsequent breach of the same or any other provisions hereof, and no waiver shall be effective unless made in writing and signed by an authorized representative of the waiving party. In the event any provision of this Statement of Agreement shall for any reason be held to be invalid, illegal or unenforceable in any respect, the remaining provisions shall remain in full force and effect. G and L each acknowledge that they have been advised to obtain, and have obtained, or have had the opportunity to obtain and have declined to do so, legal counsel to provide them (respectively) with independent advice as to the contents of this Statement of Agreement.

SIGNATURES:

_____

Discovering Agreement Provisions as an Exhibit

Exhibit B (To a Form Lease Agreement)

Vision & Values: We envision an enjoyable Lessor/Lessee relationship that is peaceful, collaborative, and mutually beneficial—one in which Lessor and Lessee can count on one another to value: safety of property and people while on the premises, responsible and conscientious care and use of the property, congenial and cooperative conduct towards one another and others, mutual fairness, responsiveness, and reasonableness.

Addressing Change and Engaging Disagreement

We each understand that there could be occurrences that no one anticipated. It is also possible that times may come when we find ourselves in disagreement over some aspect of the Lease. If something unanticipated happens or if we find ourselves in disagreement, both Lessee (name) and Lessor (name) are committed to avoiding adversarial proceedings of any kind and to seeking instead a system for collaborating to bring whatever transformation will best serve the needs of all.

Accordingly, if we find ourselves in disagreement, we each commit to dedicate our efforts towards bringing ourselves back into agreement as quickly as possible by talking together honestly, openly, in good faith, and with a commitment to a sense of fairness for all involved in accordance with our shared Vision & Values (stated above). We will focus our dialogue[6] on brainstorming ways to bring ourselves and our actions back into alignment with the stated Vision & Values that work for both of us.

If we find that we are unable to reach resolution among ourselves by informal discussion conducted in accordance with the Values and focused on serving the Vision stated in this **Exhibit B**, then we agree to attempt to resolve any dispute, claim or controversy arising out of or relating to this Lease by mediation, which shall be conducted under the then current mediation procedures of *The Center for Understanding in Conflict* or any other procedure upon which we may agree at that time.

We further agree that our respective good faith participation in mediation is a condition precedent to pursuing any other available legal or equitable remedy, including litigation, arbitration, or other dispute resolution procedures.

Either party may commence the mediation process by providing to the other party written notice, setting forth the subject of the dispute, claim or controversy, and the relief requested. Within ten (10) days after the receipt of the foregoing notice, the other party shall deliver a written response to the

---

[6] A person-to-person conversation with no preconceived outcome, listening not to refute but listening to comprehend one another's meaning, and with a willingness to be influenced and changed by what we hear.

initiating party's notice.

The initial mediation session shall be held within thirty (30) days after the initial notice. The parties agree to share equally the costs and expenses of the mediation (which shall not include the expenses incurred by each party for its own legal representation in connection with the mediation).

The parties further acknowledge and agree that mediation proceedings are settlement negotiations, and that, to the extent allowed by applicable law, all offers, promises, conduct, and statements, whether oral or written, made in the course of the mediation by any of the parties or their agents shall be confidential and inadmissible in any arbitration or other legal proceeding involving the parties; provided, however, that evidence, which is otherwise admissible or discoverable, shall not be rendered inadmissible or nondiscoverable as a result of its use in the mediation.

The provisions of this **Exhibit B** may be enforced by any Court of competent jurisdiction, and the party seeking such enforcement shall be entitled to an award of all costs, fees, and expenses, including reasonable attorneys' fees, to be paid by the party against whom enforcement is ordered.

Exhibit B Lessee Initials: _____ Lessor Initials: _____

_____

Examples of Discovering Agreement "Recitations" Used in Various Situations

(for parties who are starting a new business together in order to support a particular segment of a service industry)

Our Vision

We envision a world where [*providers of this type of services*] are free to offer [*the services*] in a manner that best suits their temperaments, talents, personalities, skills, and visions.

Our Mission

Our mission is to support inspired [*providers*] in providing quality [*services*] by empowering them to plan, implement, and grow their ideal, whole-hearted practices; and for [*Us, the Company*] to be the premier and preferred provider of [*practice*] start-up and development tools.

Our Values

We value a work setting where each of us has independence, authority, and autonomy to run our individual mission-based efforts with our teams, while others do the same. We are dedicated to kindness, respect, graciousness, and compassion towards ourselves and others in everything we do. We value innovation, courage, adaptability, excellence, and profound enjoyment.

It is important to us that we each wake up excited about the day ahead, interested in the things on our schedules, eager to begin. It is also important:

- to each have, at a minimum, enough money to comfortably cover expenses plus money for fun;
- to do our work for and in a way that creates a better world for all living beings;
- to work with people who we care deeply about and who care deeply about us and one another; and
- to have fun, laughter, and mutual support in our efforts.

Our Intent

In our collaboration, each contributor's missions are based on the desires, talents, and skills of that contributor. Collectively, our various contributory missions serve to drive our organization closer to its stated goals. Our shared Vision provides guidance to decision making during mission implementation, and our Values inform how each mission is carried out. As leaders, we will decide which missions to undertake using the governance principles and framework laid out in this Statement of Agreement so that competing ideas are managed in a way that honors and engenders creativity and harmony. Our intent is to allow a freedom of execution while keeping the organization moving in the desired direction.

———————————————————

(sale of a business to employee)

Values

We [*names of parties*] value a work setting and relationship where each of us has independence, authority, and autonomy to manage our individual efforts with our teams, while others do the same. We are dedicated to kindness, respect, graciousness, and compassion towards ourselves and others in everything we do. We value reliability, adaptability, excellence, and enjoyment. We also deeply value our friendship and come to this arrangement from a genuine desire to create an endeavor that benefits the well-being of each and every one of us. We commit to one another that we will make every effort to conduct our interactions in a manner that places mutual well-being as our top priority and serves our understanding that we are joining forces in this endeavor so that our shared energies and abilities can be harnessed to generate greater well-being for each and every one of us.

Intent

It is our shared goal for [*person A*] to become a business owner in her own right and to continue to carry forward the [*Company*] tradition and product line. [*Persons B&C*] intend to produce [*certain product lines*] in support of that goal for at least five years.

(excerpts from a publishing agreement)

Exhibit A

Vision, Mission, Values Statements

The following statements express the parties' core, underlying interests in connection with this shared endeavor. They represent the vision(s) we hold that motivate us to persevere in our work, the mission(s) we are joining forces to accomplish, the constraints and imperatives that inform our decision making, and the values with which we want to align all our actions.

The statements are meant to serve as reference points to orient and focus our conversations in support of creative and productive, collaborative problem solving should we find ourselves in disagreement in the course of our relationship and work together.

* * *

Author's Constraints & Imperatives for This Endeavor

Financial and personal well-being. I must maintain the level of income that is required for the financial well-being of my family and myself. Currently, I do this with my solo legal and business consulting practices. I also must maintain a healthy work/rest balance while pursuing financial well-being. I'll be considering carefully how the publishing relationship and project impact the health of my practices, income streams, and work/ rest balance.

Ideological integrity. This work and message involve a

profound change of paradigm. Cultural conditioning and conventional practices can create blind spots and back pressure against the shift required to bring transformation. An awareness of the nuances in language and practice that tend to subvert the paradigm shift is required. I'll be fiercely vigilant about clarity and integrity of message and meaning in the book and related activities.

Examples of ACED Provisions Used in Various Situations

(between Customer/Consultant Service)

How We Will Address Change[7]

From time to time, circumstances may change. New information may come to light. The change may emerge slowly or something sudden and unexpected may happen. The change may be positive or challenging. We may need to make changes to our agreement in the middle of the term. Our intention is to work together effectively and gracefully through all kinds of change. When issues arise, we commit to having a conversation to examine how to handle change and keep the relationship on track.

We will base our conversations on our mutual commitment to staying in alignment with the values and agreements in this document.

The following questions can also be used to help figure out a

---

[7] Adapted from materials provided by J. Kim Wright.

way forward:

1. Does each of us feel we are getting what we anticipated? Is there something that is no longer working for one or both of us?
2. What do we most appreciate about the work we have done together so far?
3. Are there outside influences (or money) affecting how we are working together?
4. What has really worked well for us so far? How can we expand on it?
5. Is it time to redefine or redirect our work together?
6. Is there something difficult we are avoiding saying or doing?
7. What do we gain by continuing/ending this work together?

The biggest tragedy that we could imagine is that an unresolvable conflict would arise that would cause either of us to instigate litigation. We will do everything in our power to avoid that possibility. We intend and commit that all disputes will be settled without intervention by the adversarial court system. It is our intention to use dispute resolution models that are focused on our shared values to resolve any conflict.

If these questions/conversations cannot get us back on track, then we will seek assistance in the form of:

a. **Mediation** is a process through which we choose a neutral facilitator to help us discuss our issues. The Mediator does not represent either of us or give us legal advice. It is most helpful when communication and brainstorming are most likely to reach an outcome.
b. **Collaborative Law** is a process in which we consult two specially trained lawyers. Collaborative lawyers enter into a contract to provide legal advice, problem-solving skills and facilitation to achieve an agreement, but will

not go to court. This approach is useful if there are legal issues that need expertise.

If our chosen option is still not successful in restoring us to agreement, we choose the option of Termination, completing the work to a certain point and ending the relationship gracefully.

EXCEPTION: Protecting intellectual property rights

ACME Company retains the right to take whatever legal action ACME deems necessary to protect and prevent infringement of ACME's intellectual property including, but not limited to, seeking injunctive relief without delay.

Customer also retains the right to take whatever legal action Customer deems necessary to protect and prevent infringement of Customer's intellectual property including, but not limited to, seeking injunctive relief without delay.

Terminating the Agreement

Either Party may terminate this Agreement in whole or in part for convenience and without cause at any time by giving the other Party at least 30 (thirty) days prior written notice designating the termination date. The Customer agrees to pay for any products delivered or services rendered at the time of termination.

(from a speaker's agreement)

Addressing Change & Engaging Disagreement

The following statements are meant to serve as reference points to orient and focus our conversations in support of creative and productive, collaborative problem solving should we find ourselves in disagreement in the course of our relationship and work together.

- **Vision**—I envision a world where people make decisions about what they want (and what will happen when they get it) on the basis of a realistic understanding of the costs and benefits—a world where people engage success and its disruptions as natural, normal, and predictable.
- **Mission**—In service of this vision, my mission is to put language to people's experience of success and its aftermath, and thereby reduce the damage that is often caused by how people deal with success. My mission is to help people learn to use success as a catalyst and a vehicle for personal development.
- **Values**—I value fun, learning, collaboration, colleagueship, non-exacting, flexibility, synergy, generosity, and keeping a sense of humor.

Why We Are Choosing to Work Together

I am choosing to work with you because doing so aligns with my vision of a better world and my mission for helping to bring that vision into being. You are choosing to work with me because your vision, mission, and values align with mine; and you believe the audience you are bringing together for my presentation will benefit from the perspective, support, and inspiration that I can offer based on my profession and personal experience.

Creative Conflict

We both understand that it is possible there will be occurrences that no one anticipated. It is also possible that times may come when we find ourselves in disagreement over some aspect of our relationship or the work related to this Statement of Agreement. If something unanticipated happens or if we find ourselves in disagreement, both you and I are committed to avoiding adversarial proceedings of any kind and to collaborating to bring whatever transformation will best serve the needs of all.

Accordingly, if we find ourselves in disagreement, we each commit to dedicate our efforts towards bringing ourselves back into agreement as quickly as possible by talking together honestly, openly, in good faith, and with a commitment to finding a way forward that accords with the Vision, Mission, Values (VMV) stated above and that works for both of us. The party that feels the need to call this type of conversation will begin by providing to the other party a brief statement of the action/inaction that has triggered the request for the conversation, a statement of why the action/ inaction appears to be out of alignment with the agreed VMV and/or terms of this Agreement, and suggesting a time and place for the conversation. We'll open any such conversation by first rereading together the VMV stated in this agreement, reminding ourselves of the particular action/inaction which has triggered the request for a conversation; and we will focus on brainstorming ways to bring ourselves and our actions back into alignment with the stated VMV.

If we find that we are unable to design resolution among ourselves by informal discussion conducted in accordance with the Values and focused on serving the Vision and Mission as stated above, then we agree to attempt to resolve any dispute, claim, or controversy arising out of or relating to this Statement of Agreement by mediation, which shall be conducted under the then current mediation procedures of The Center for Understanding in Conflict or any other joint-session mediation procedure upon which we may agree at that time.

We further agree that our respective good faith participation in mediation is a condition precedent to pursuing any other available legal or equitable remedy, including litigation, arbitration, or other dispute resolution procedures; *the sole exception to this condition precedent being:* either party may seek injunctive relief without delay if that party, in their sole discretion, believes such action is needed to protect that party's intellectual property.

Surviving Terms

The terms and conditions of Sections 2, 5, and 8 shall survive termination of this Statement of Agreement.

CPSIA information can be obtained
at www.ICGtesting.com
Printed in the USA
LVHW051627110721
692416LV00010B/890

9 780999 329207